COPYRIGHT

ISBN 978-0-9899130-5-8

Thomas Ray Publishing LLC
thomasraypublishing@gmail.com

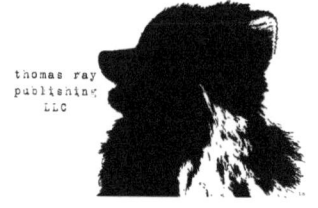

thomas ray
publishing
LLC

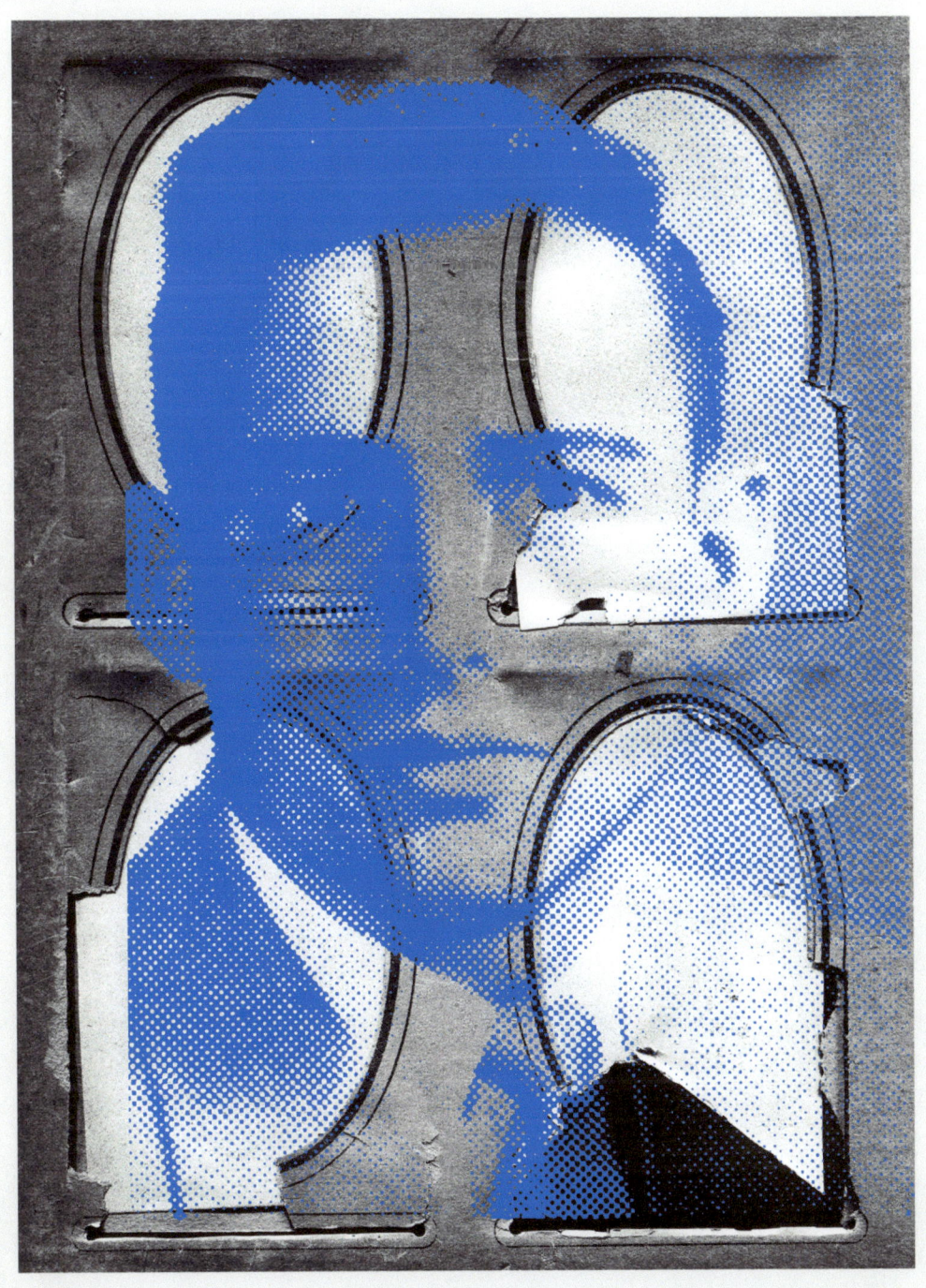

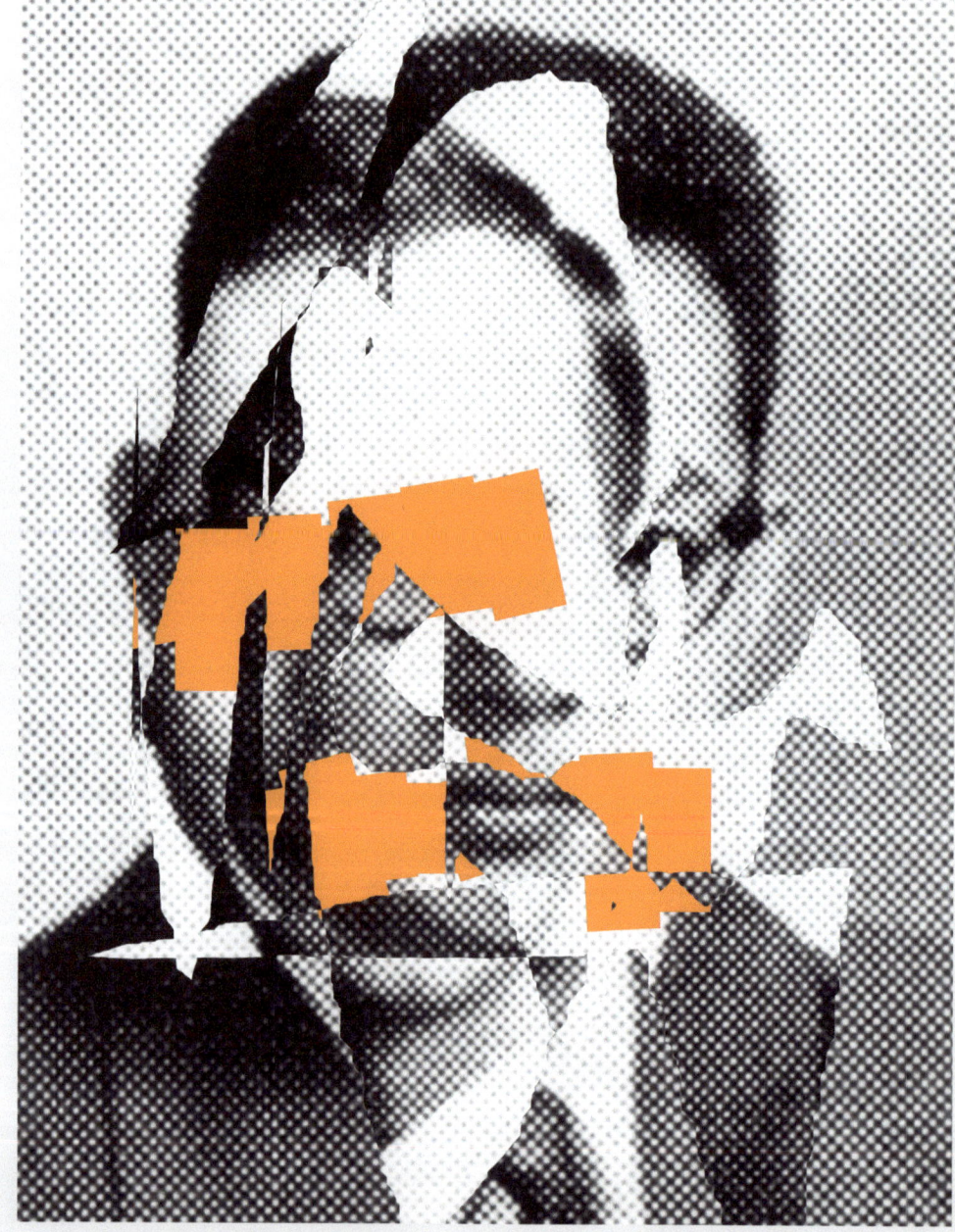

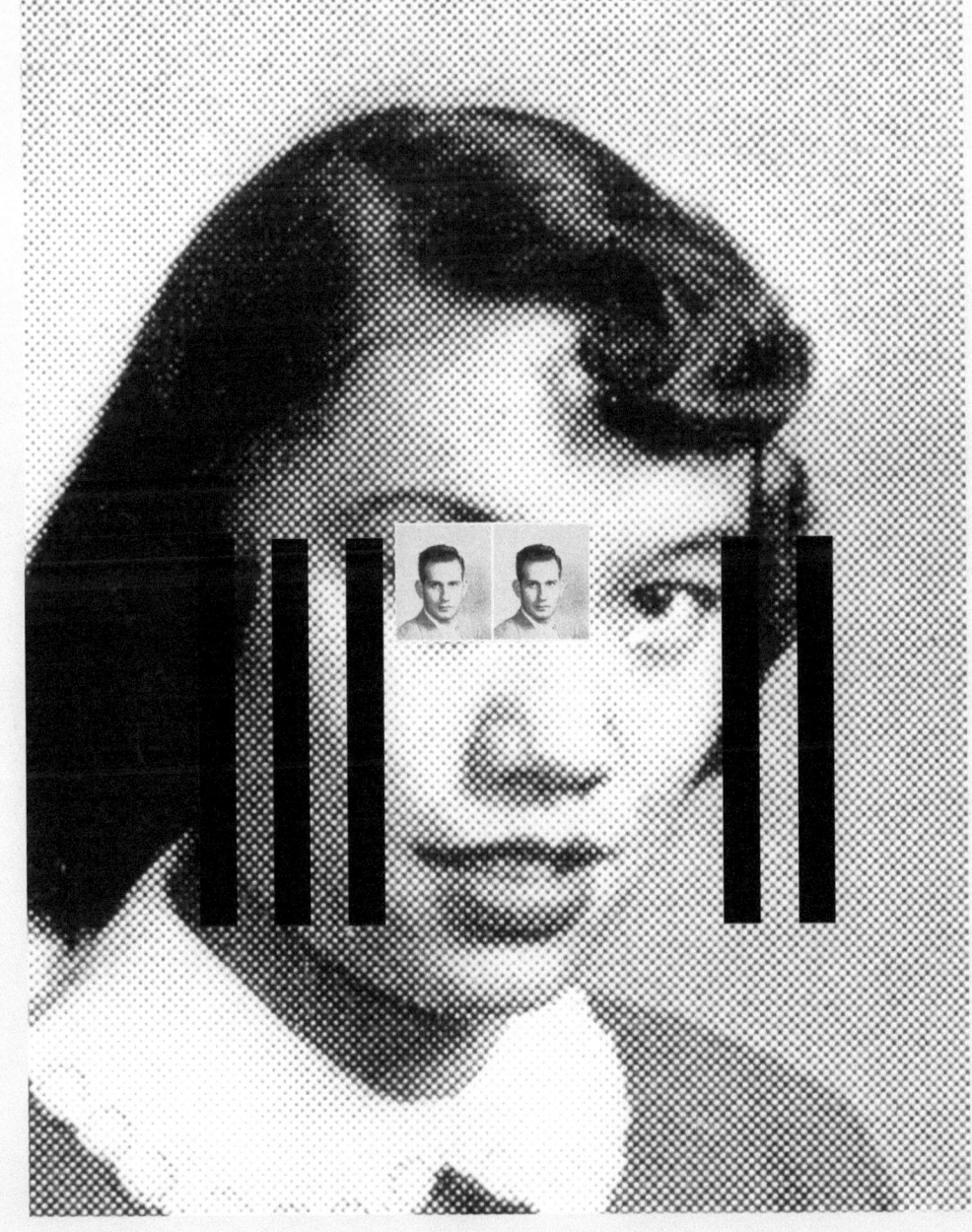

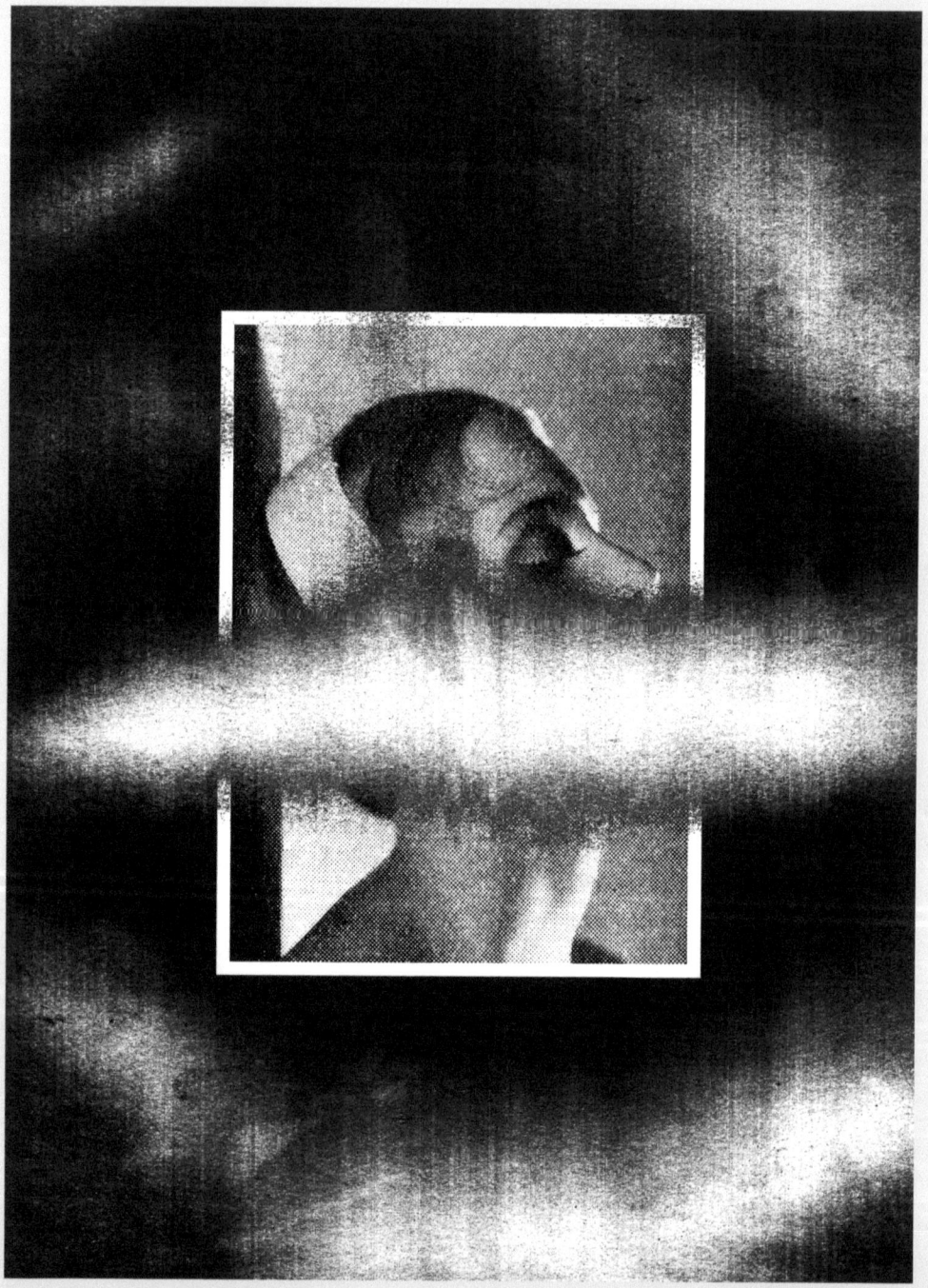

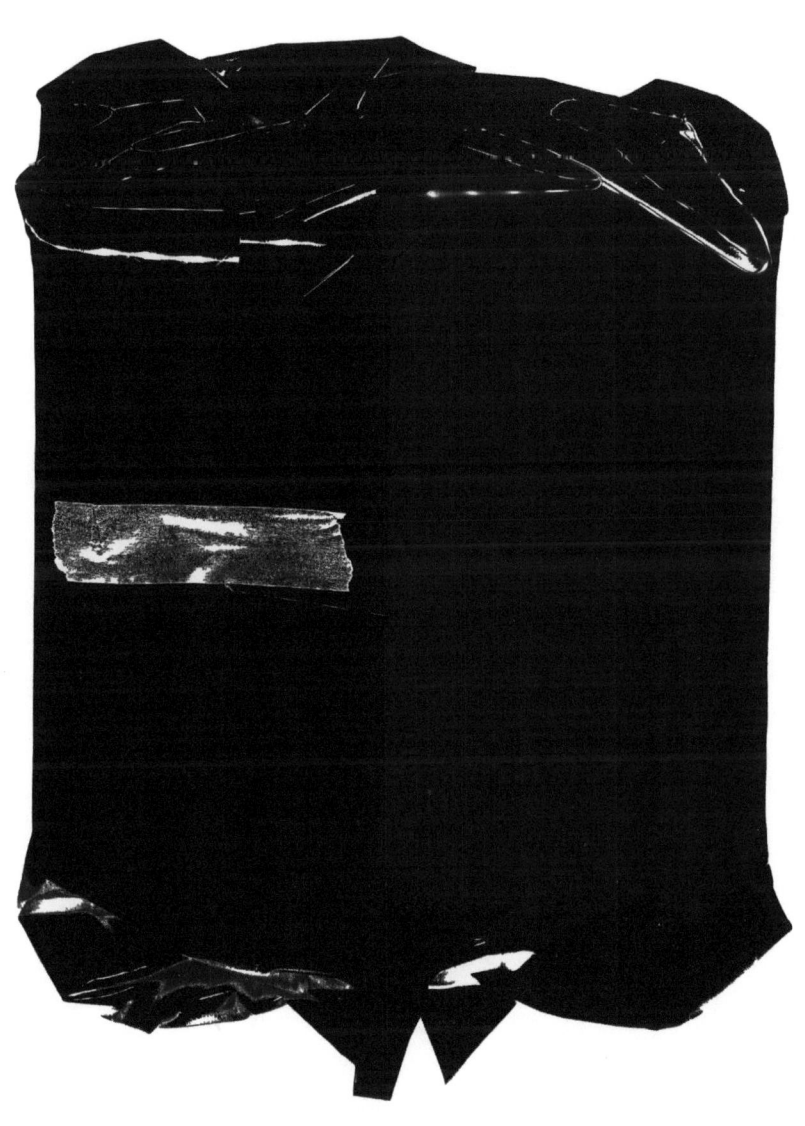

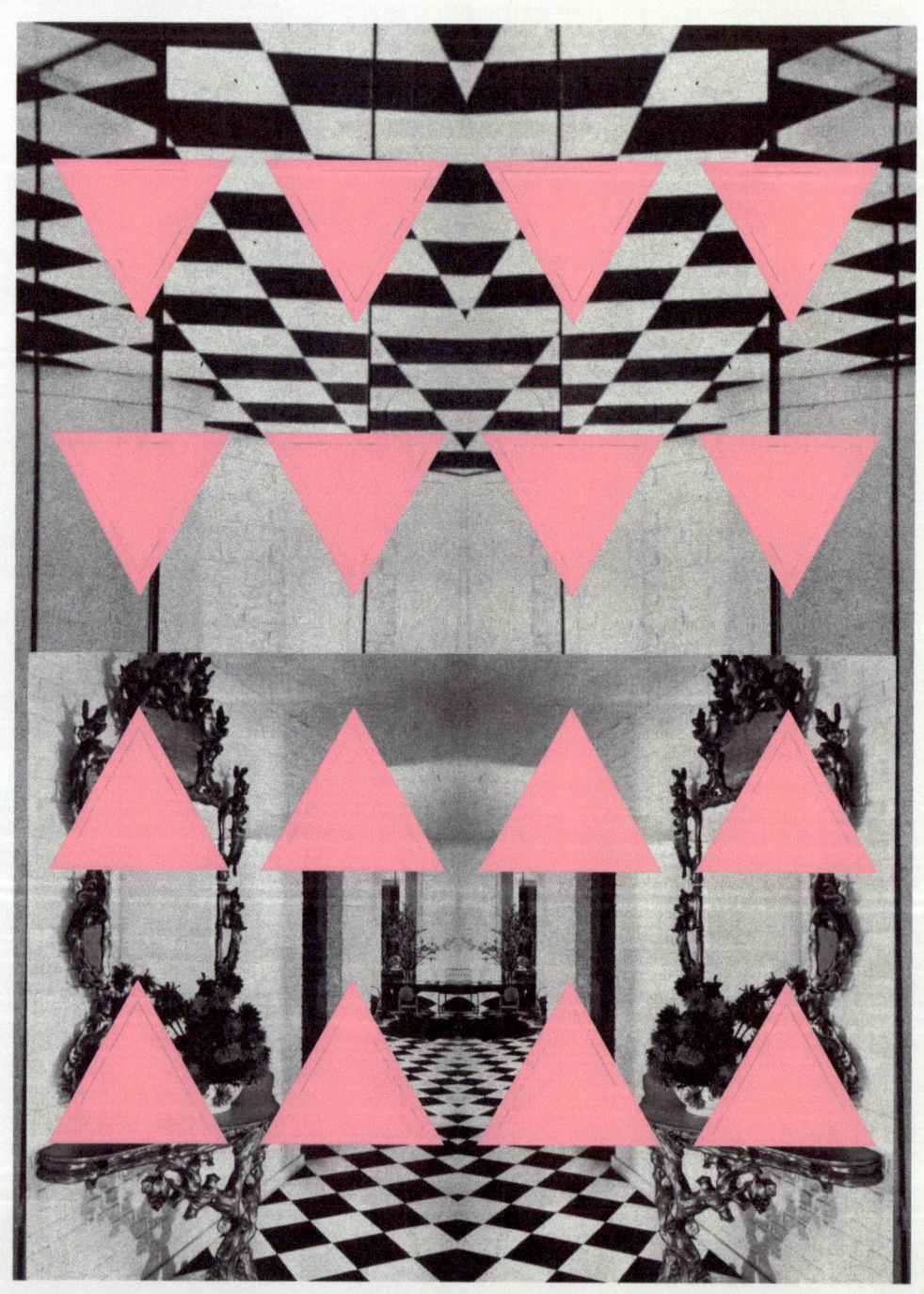

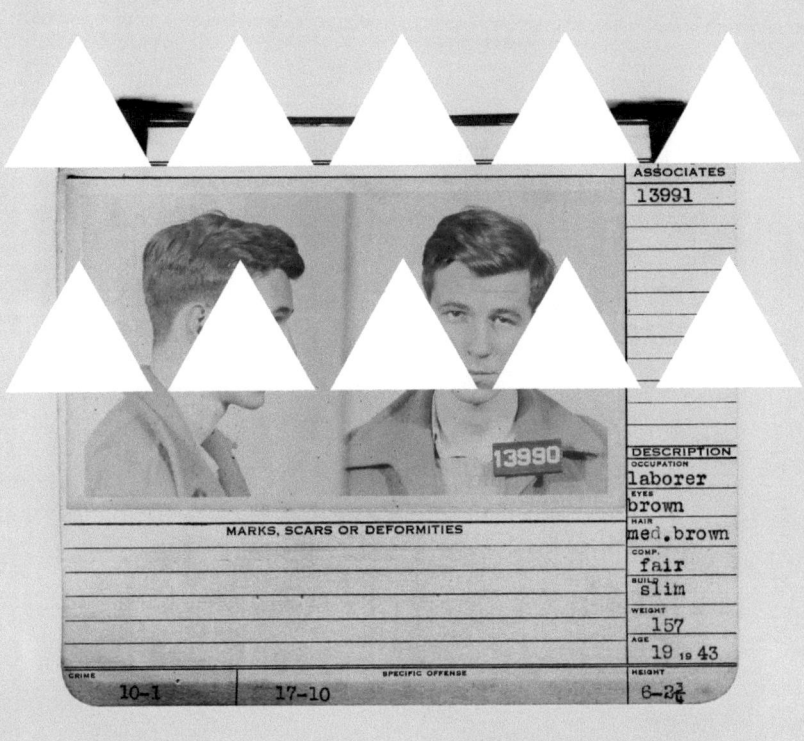

ASSOCIATES
13991

DESCRIPTION
OCCUPATION
laborer
EYES
brown
HAIR
med.brown
COMP.
fair
BUILD
slim
WEIGHT
157
AGE
19 19 43

MARKS, SCARS OR DEFORMITIES

CRIME   SPECIFIC OFFENSE   HEIGHT
10-1   17-10   6-23

13990

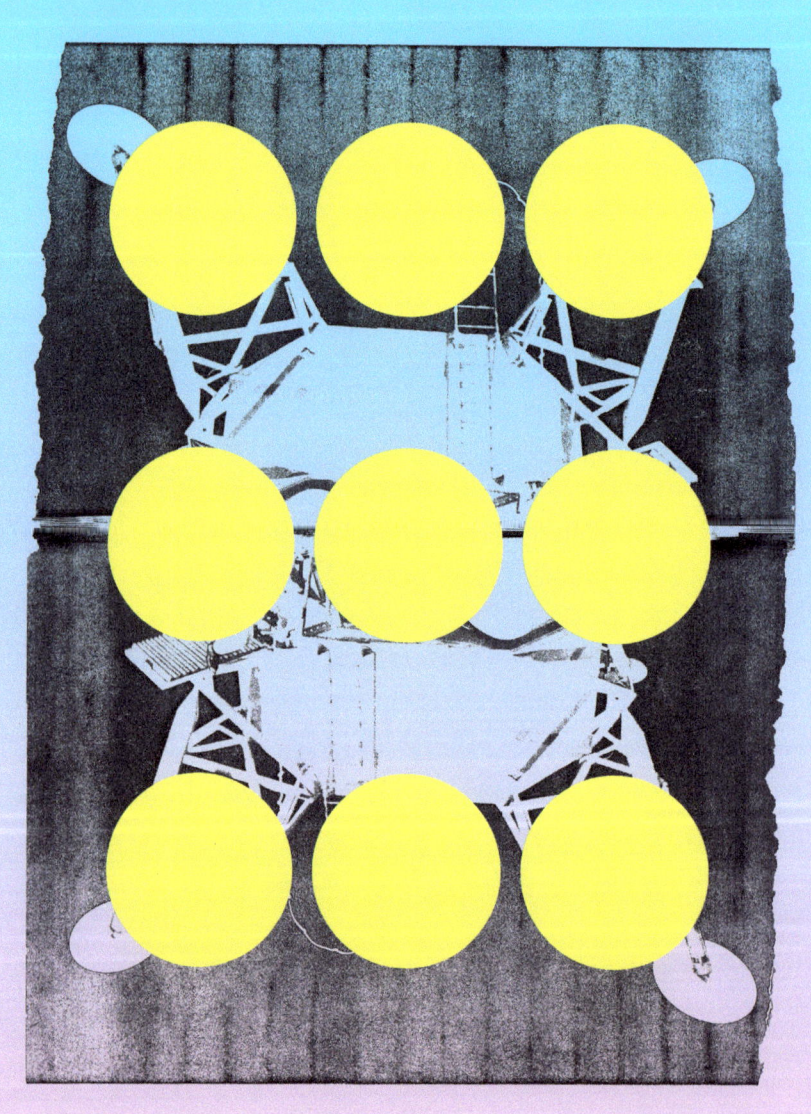

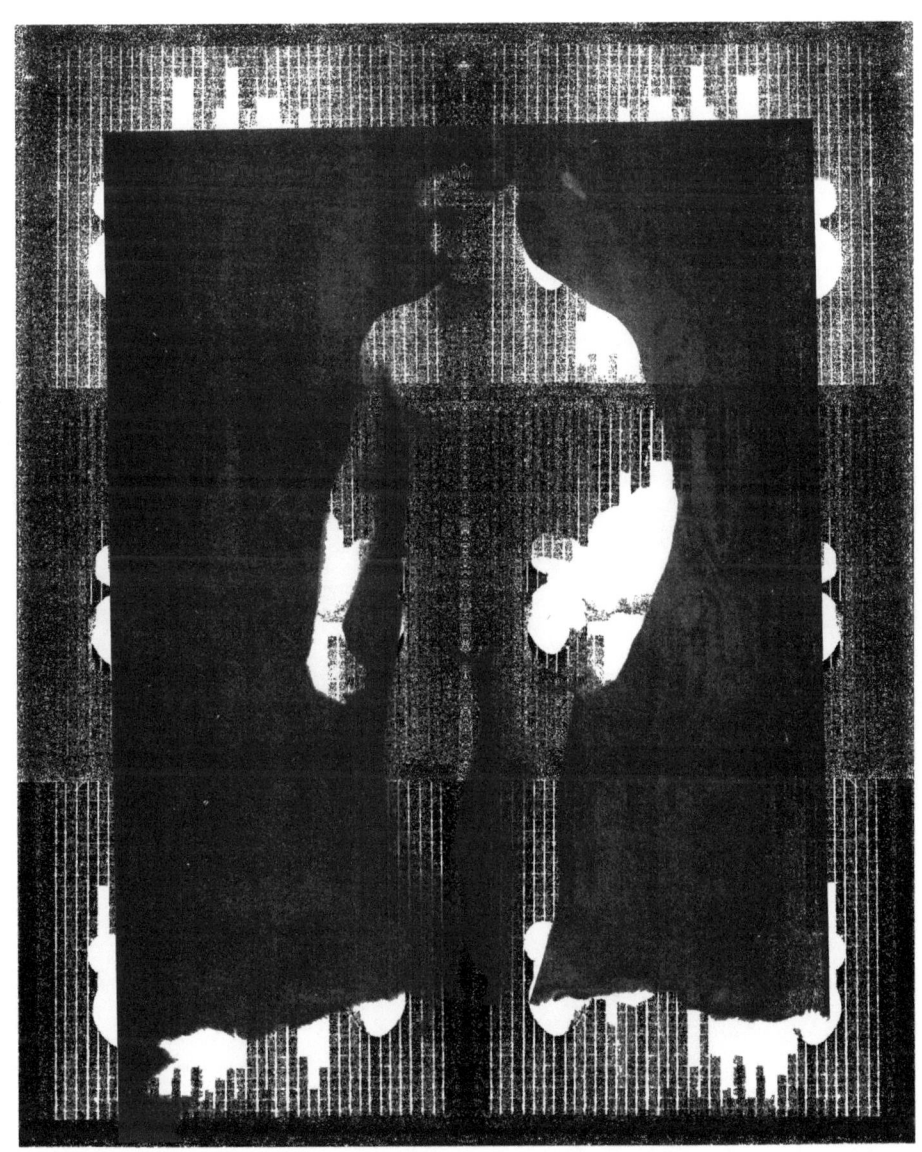

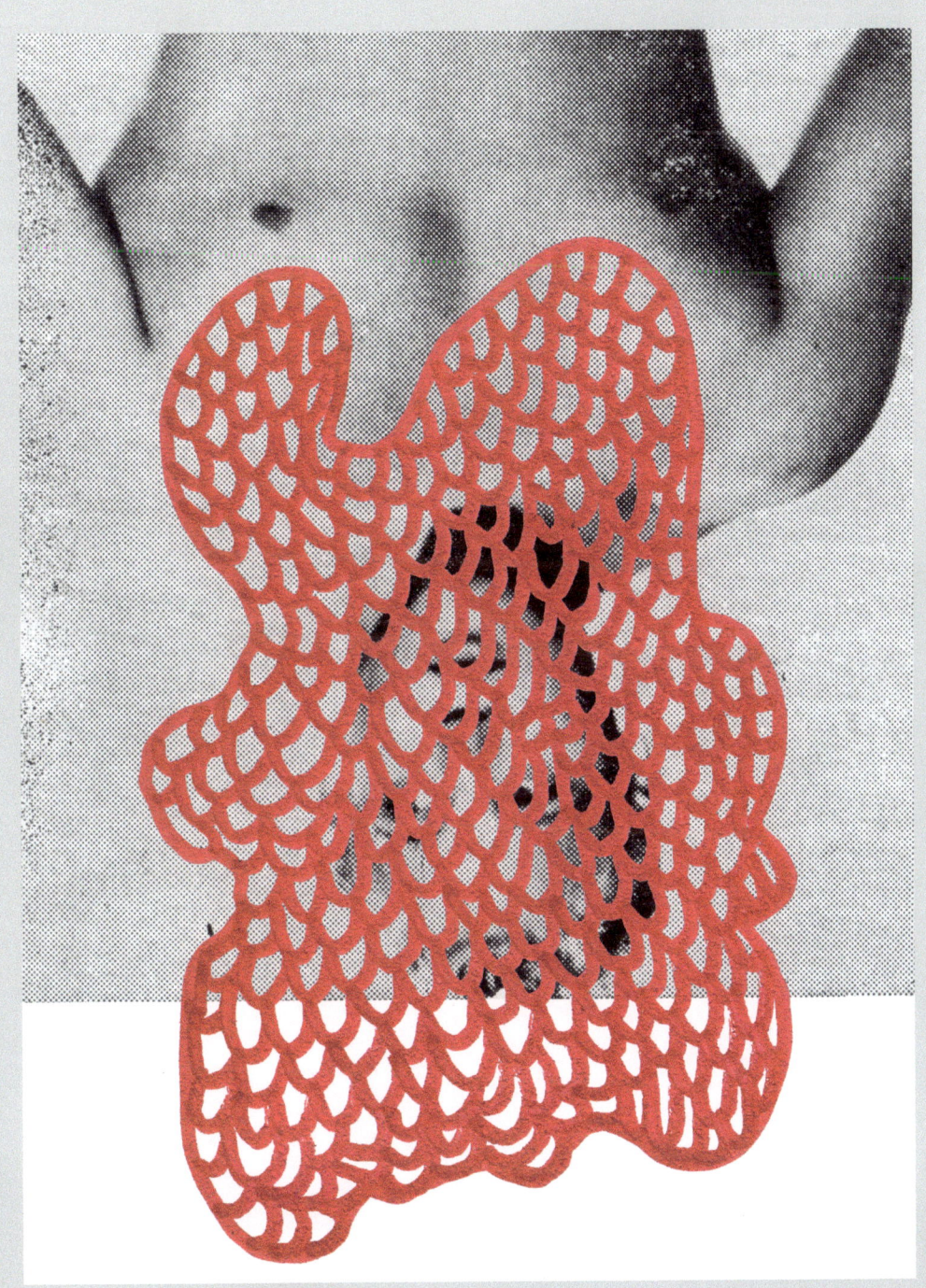

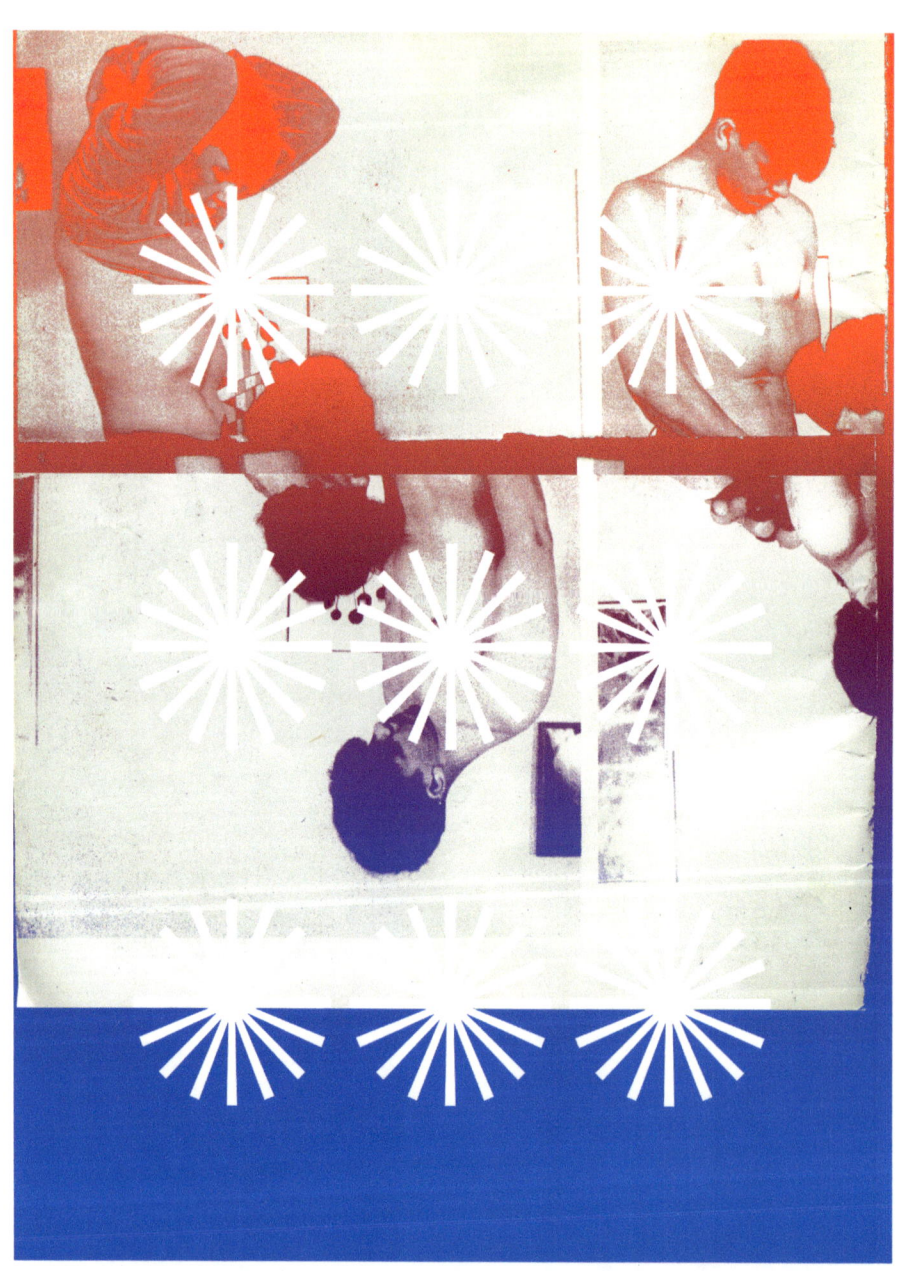

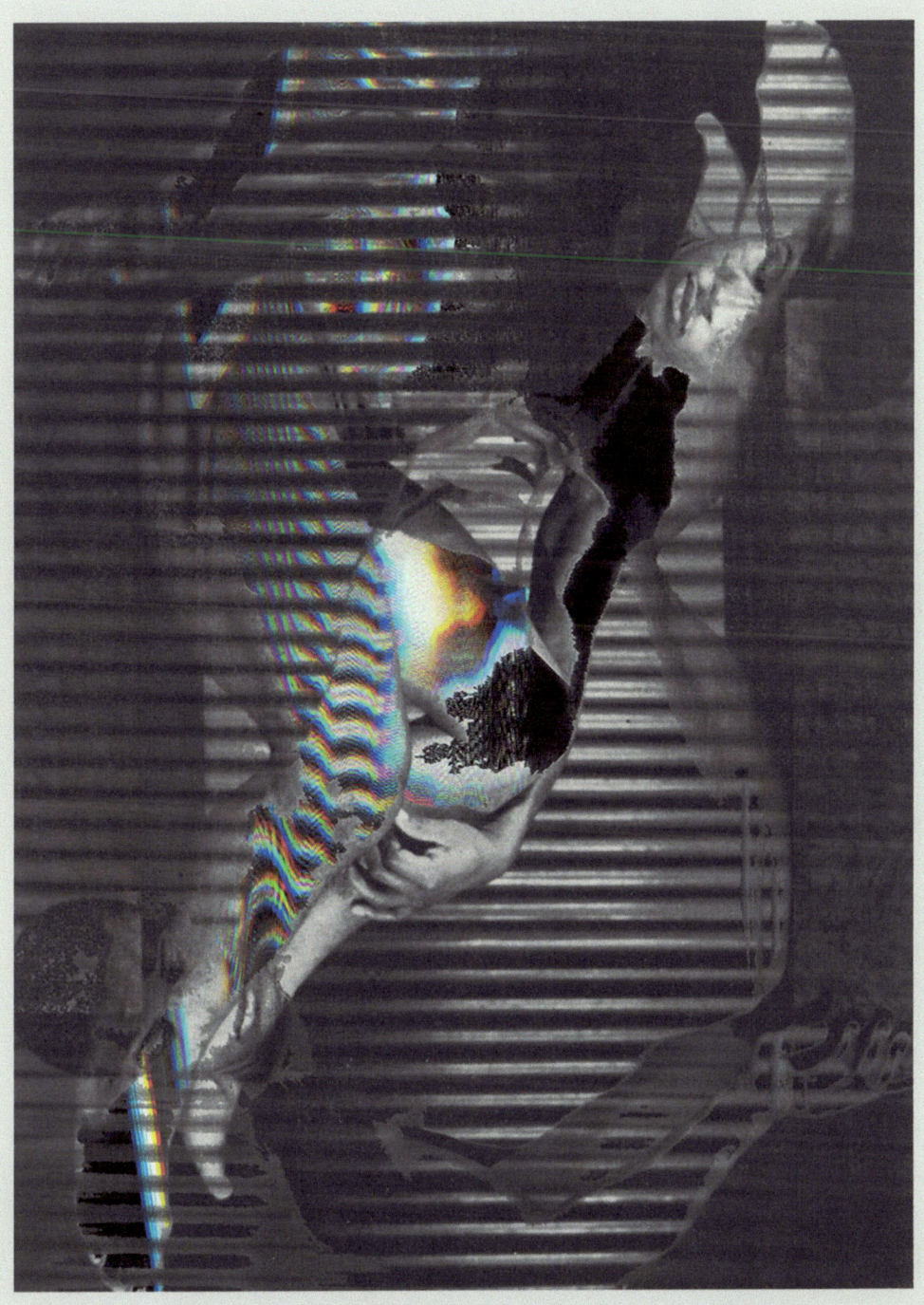

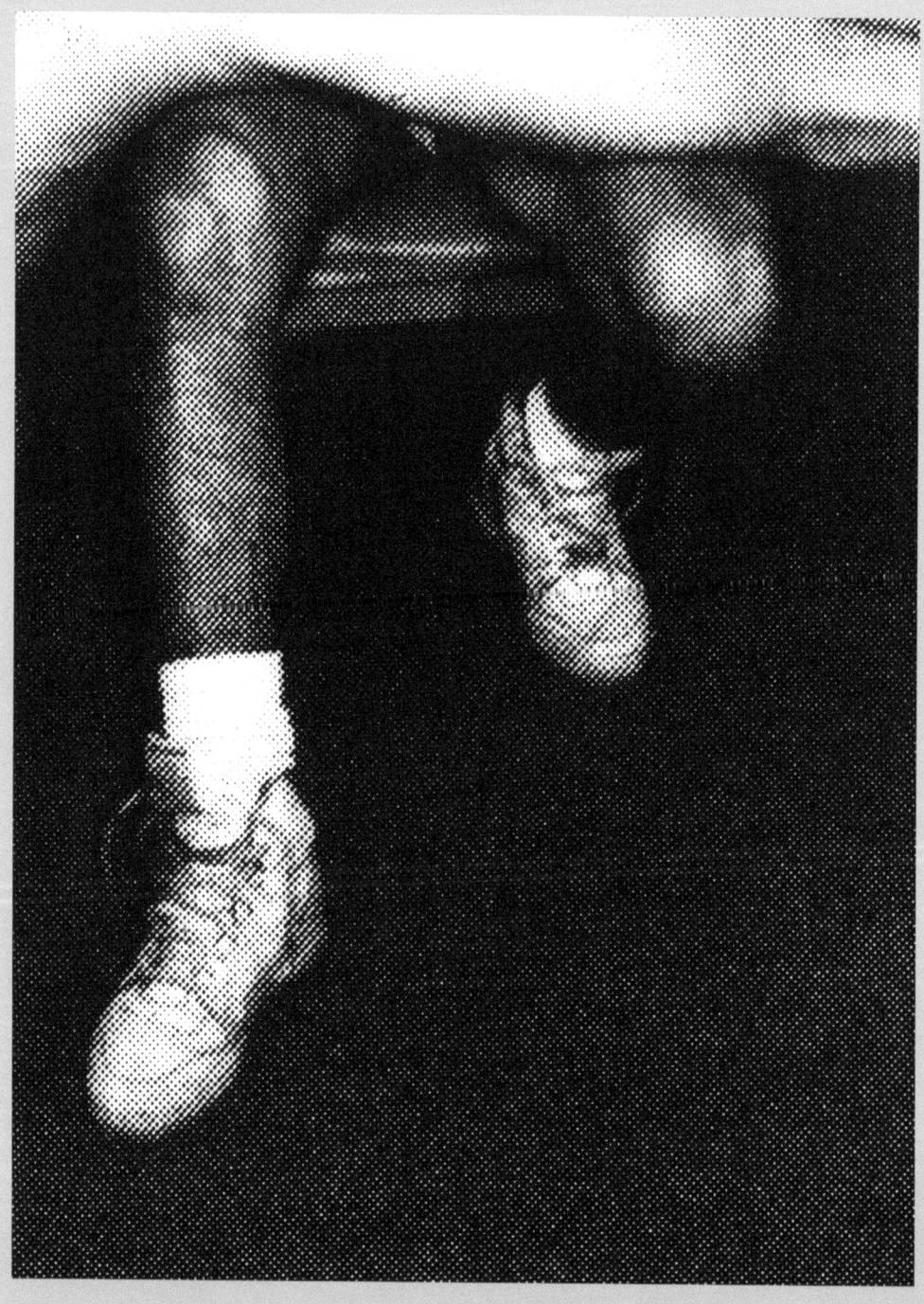

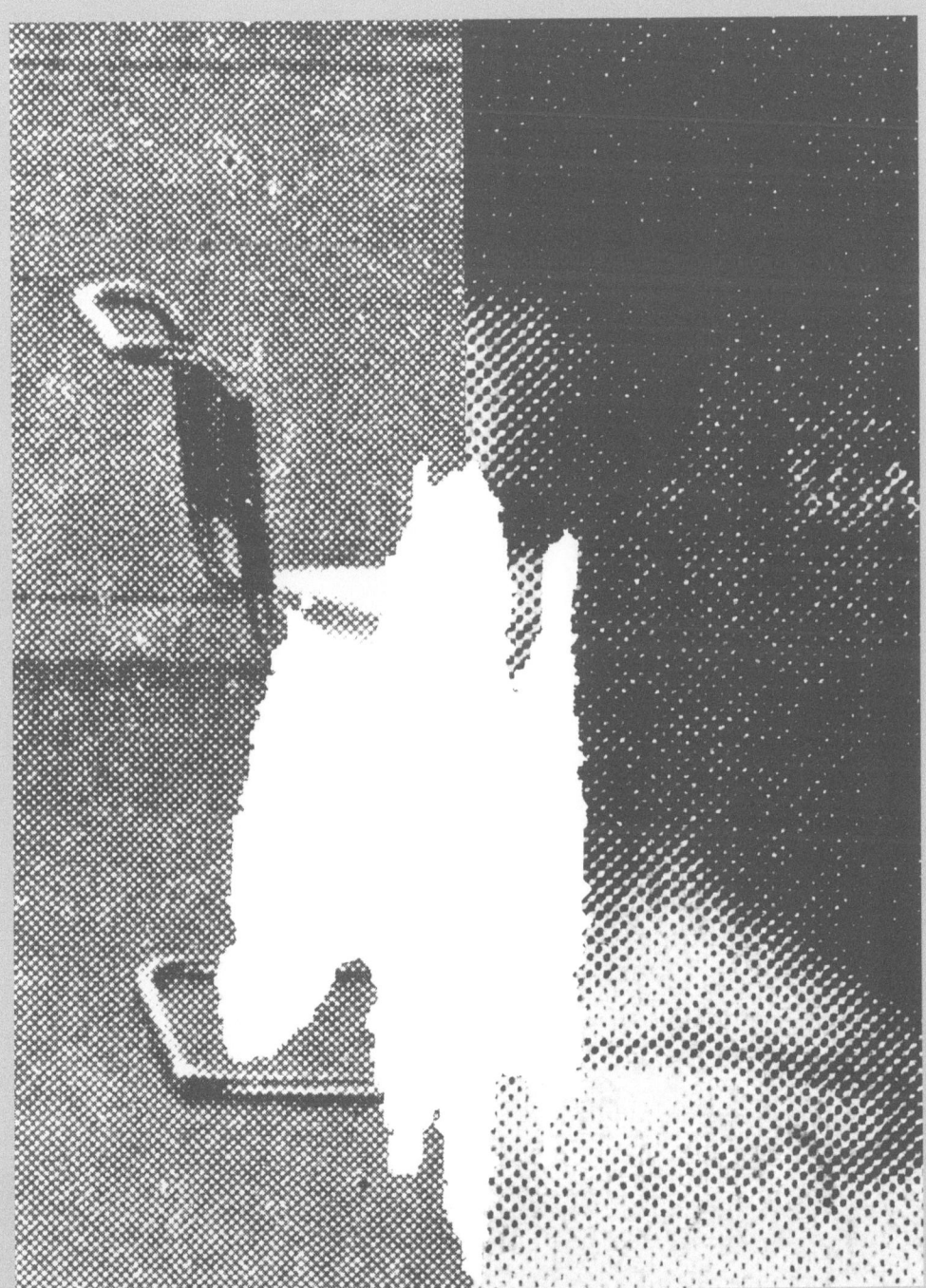

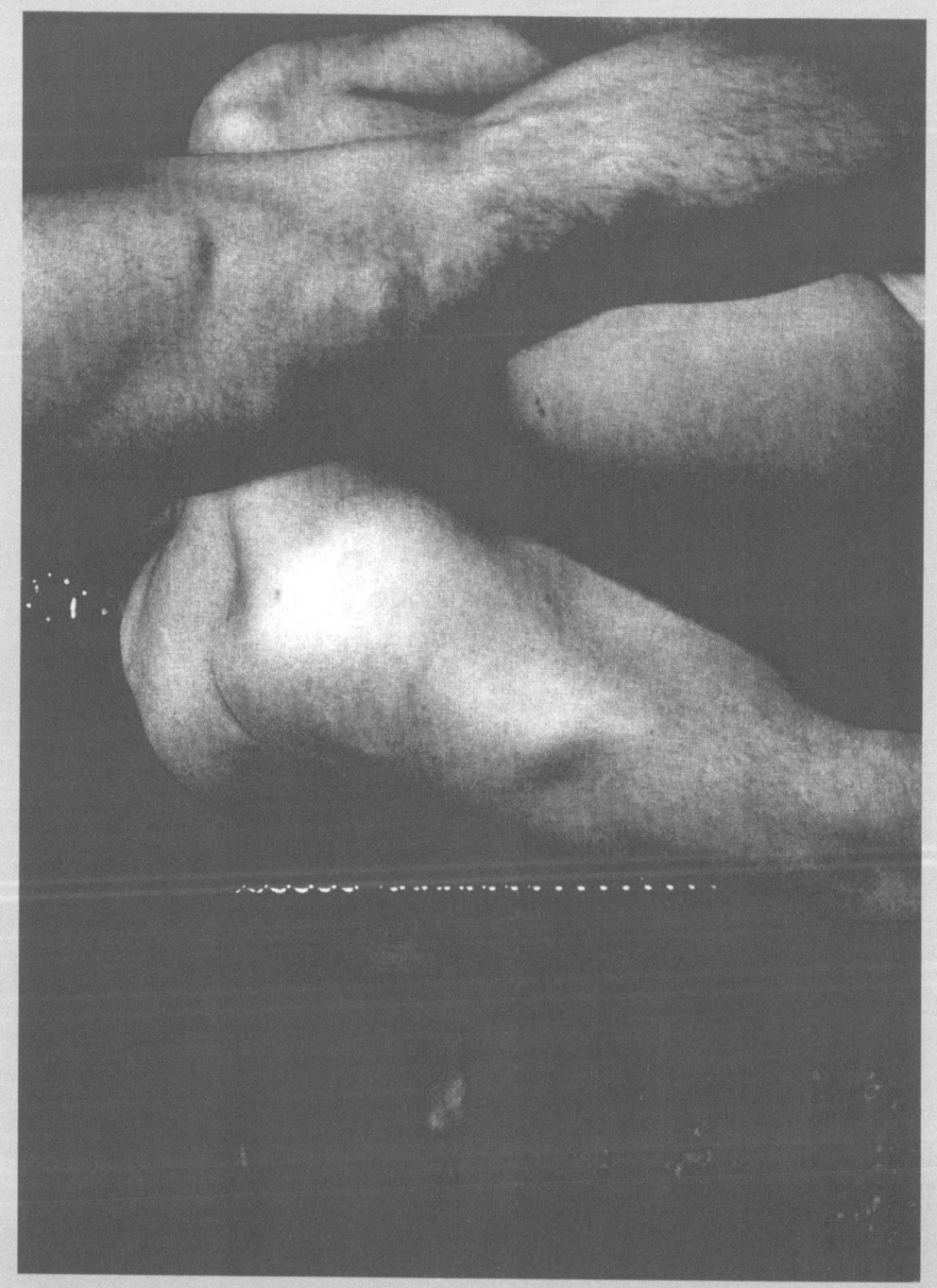

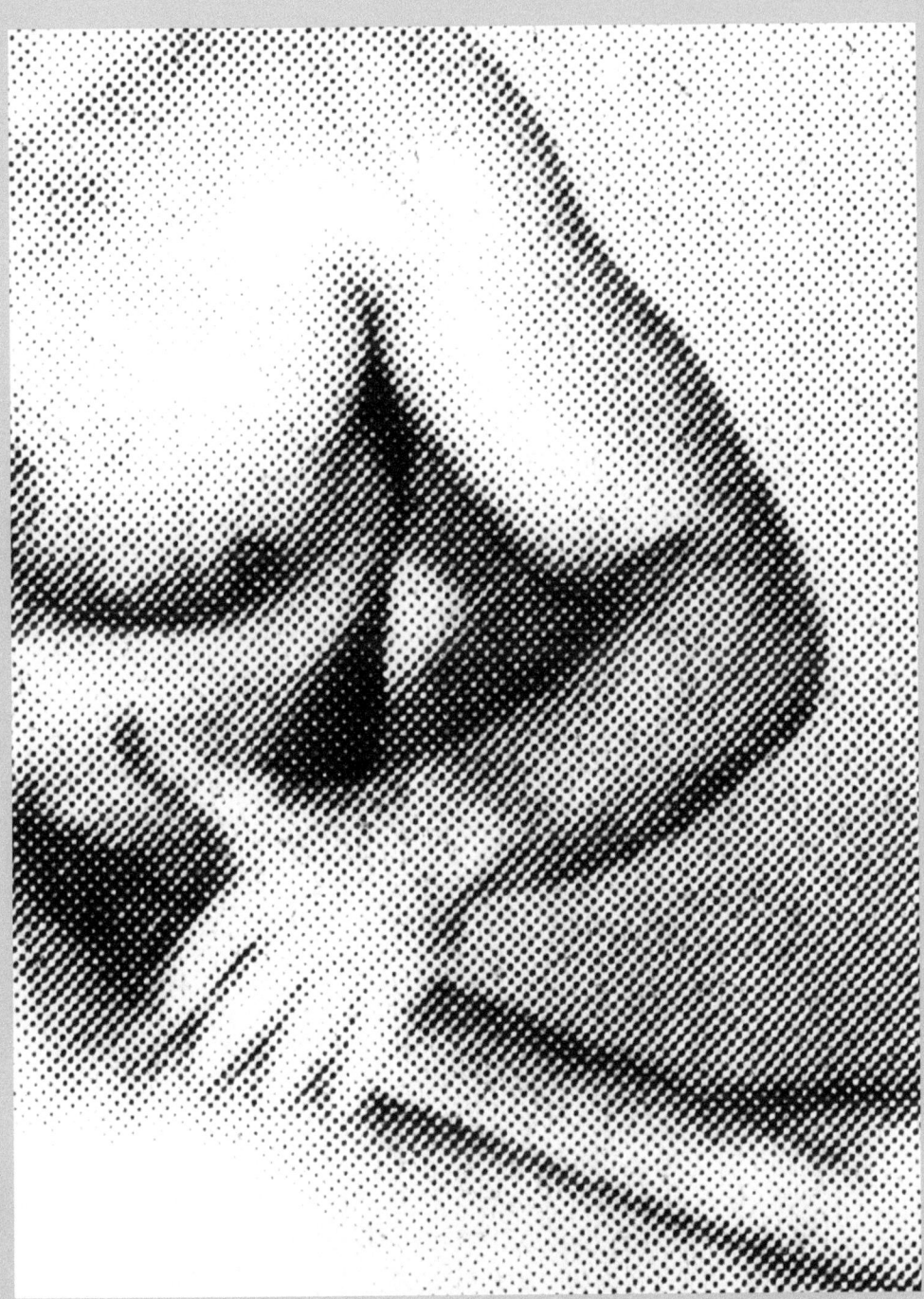

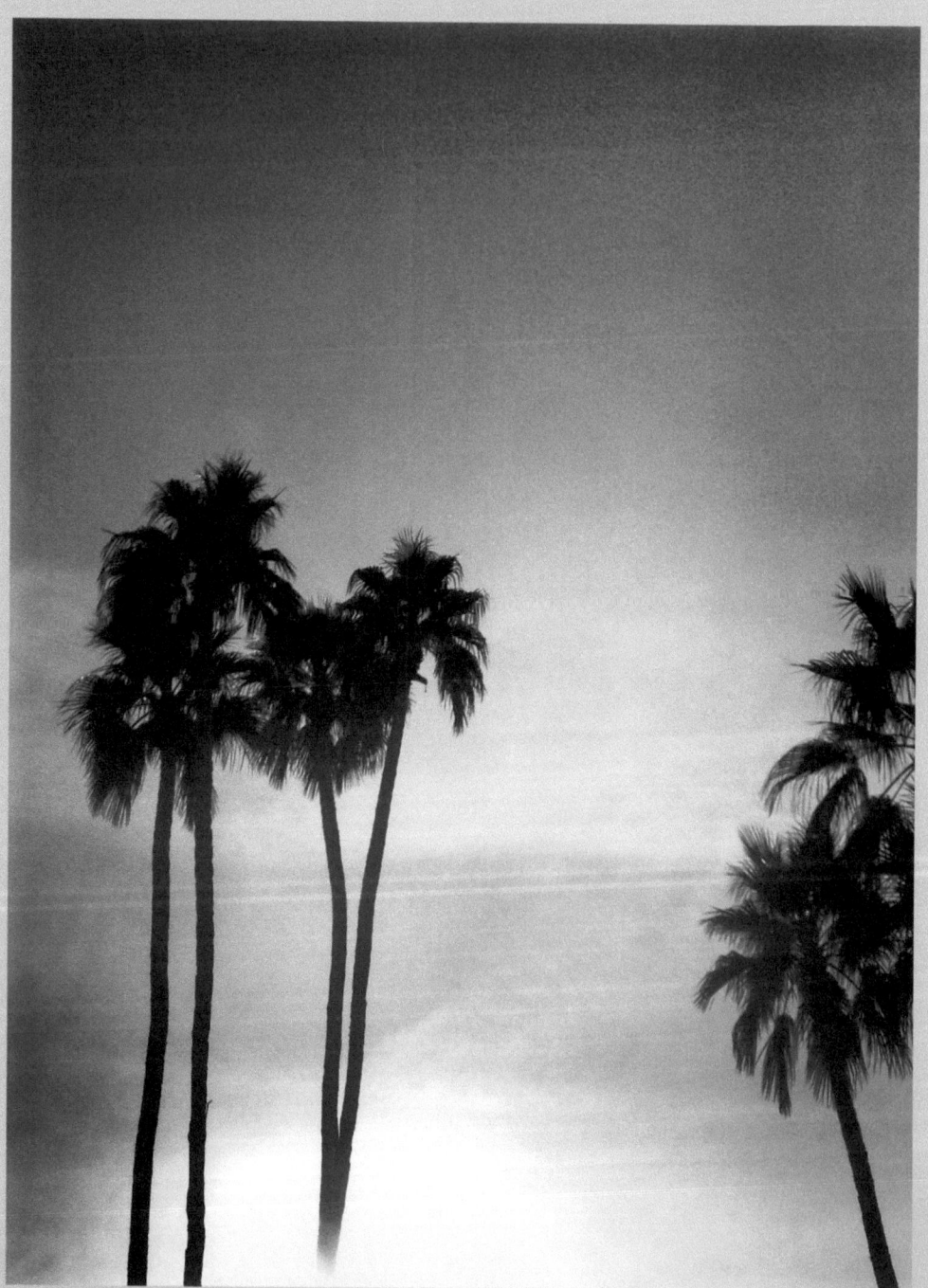

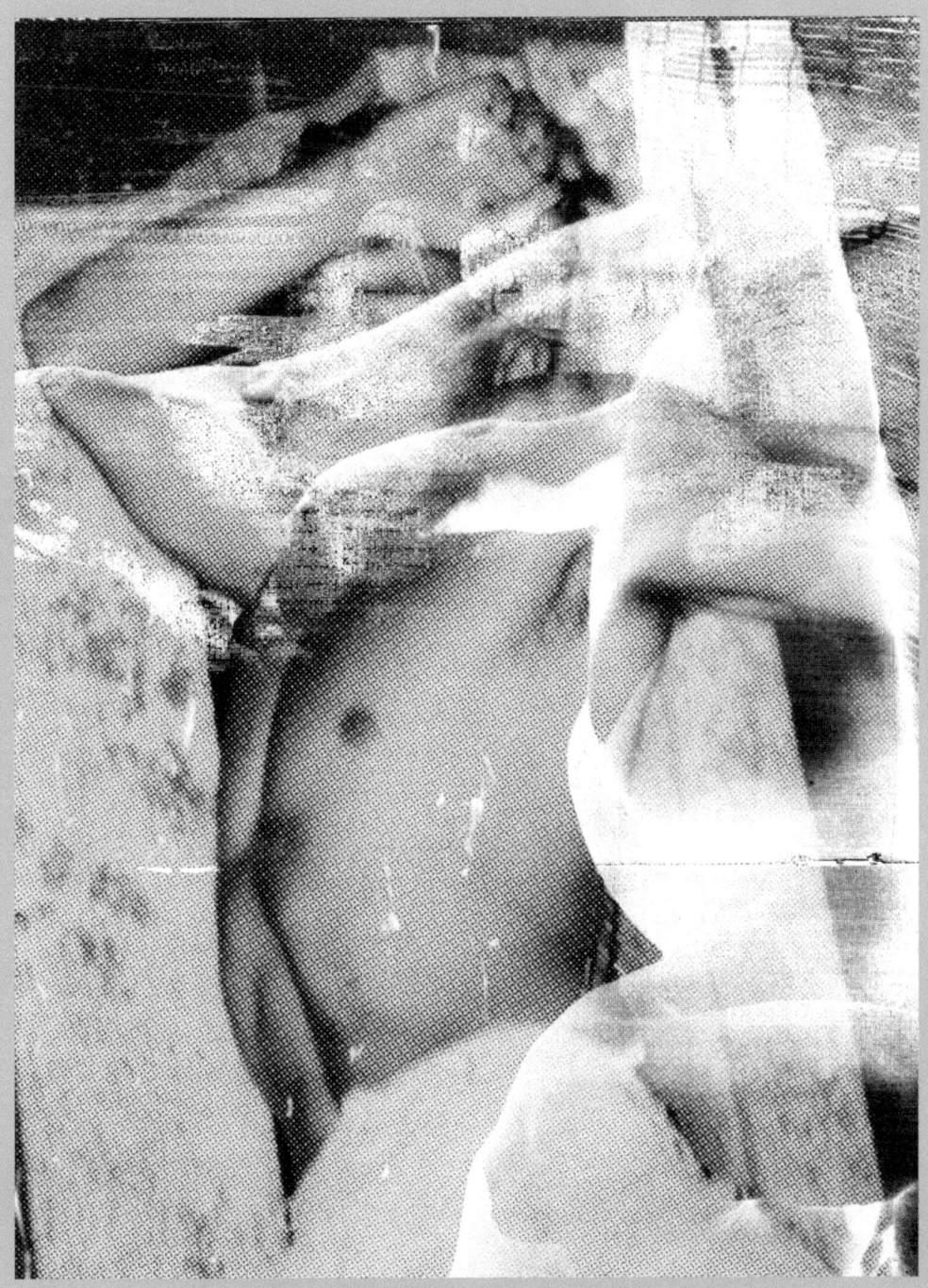

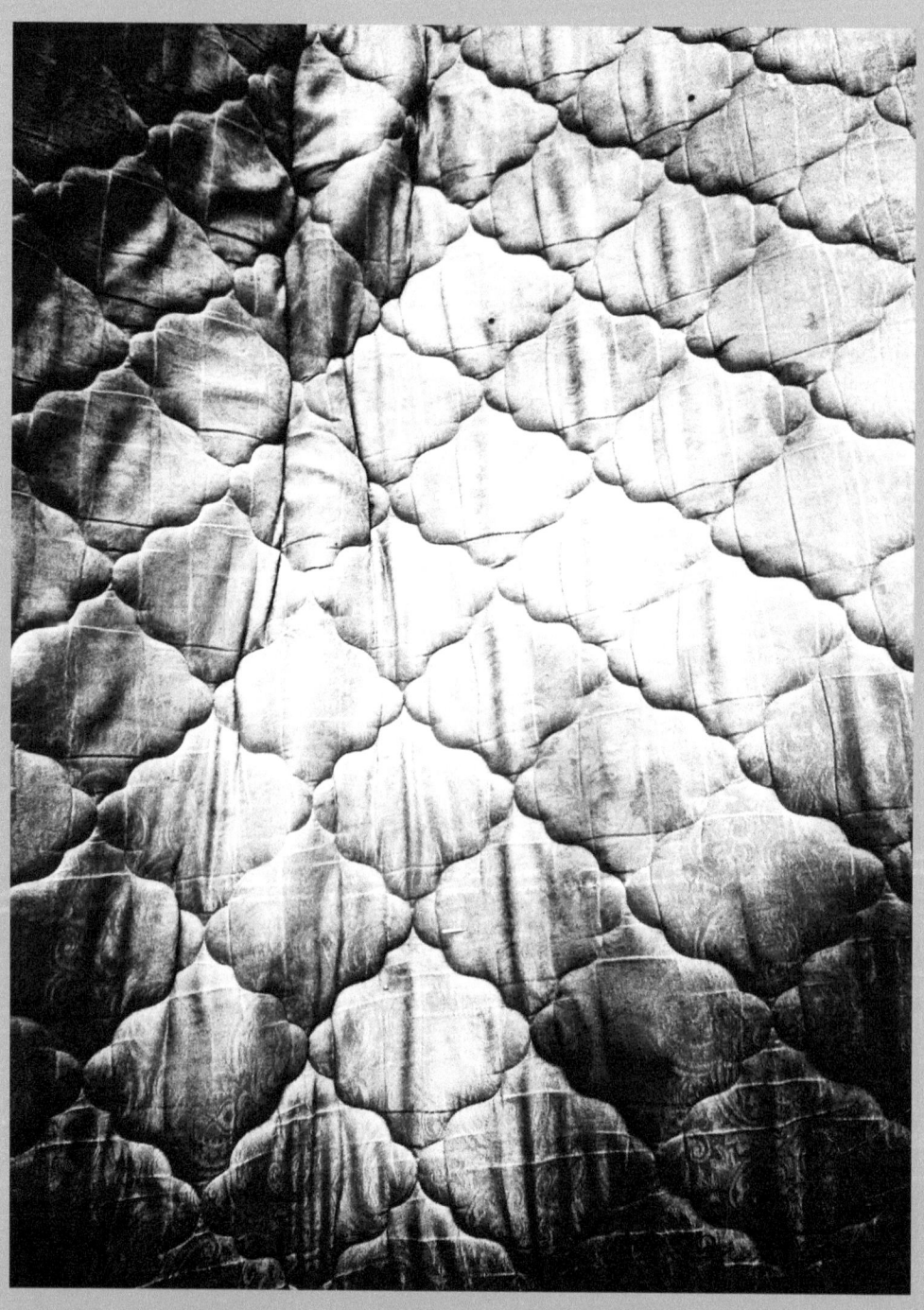

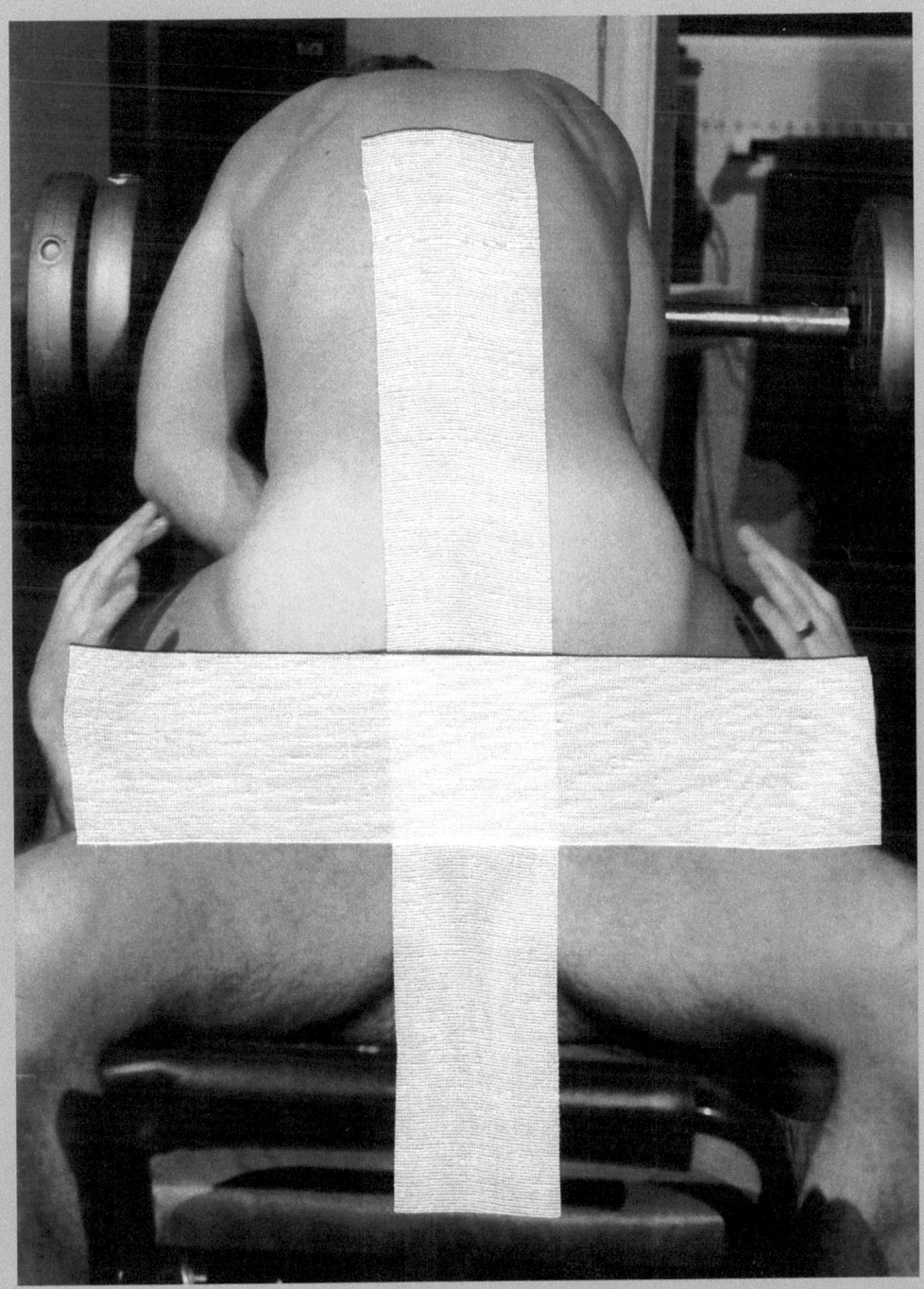

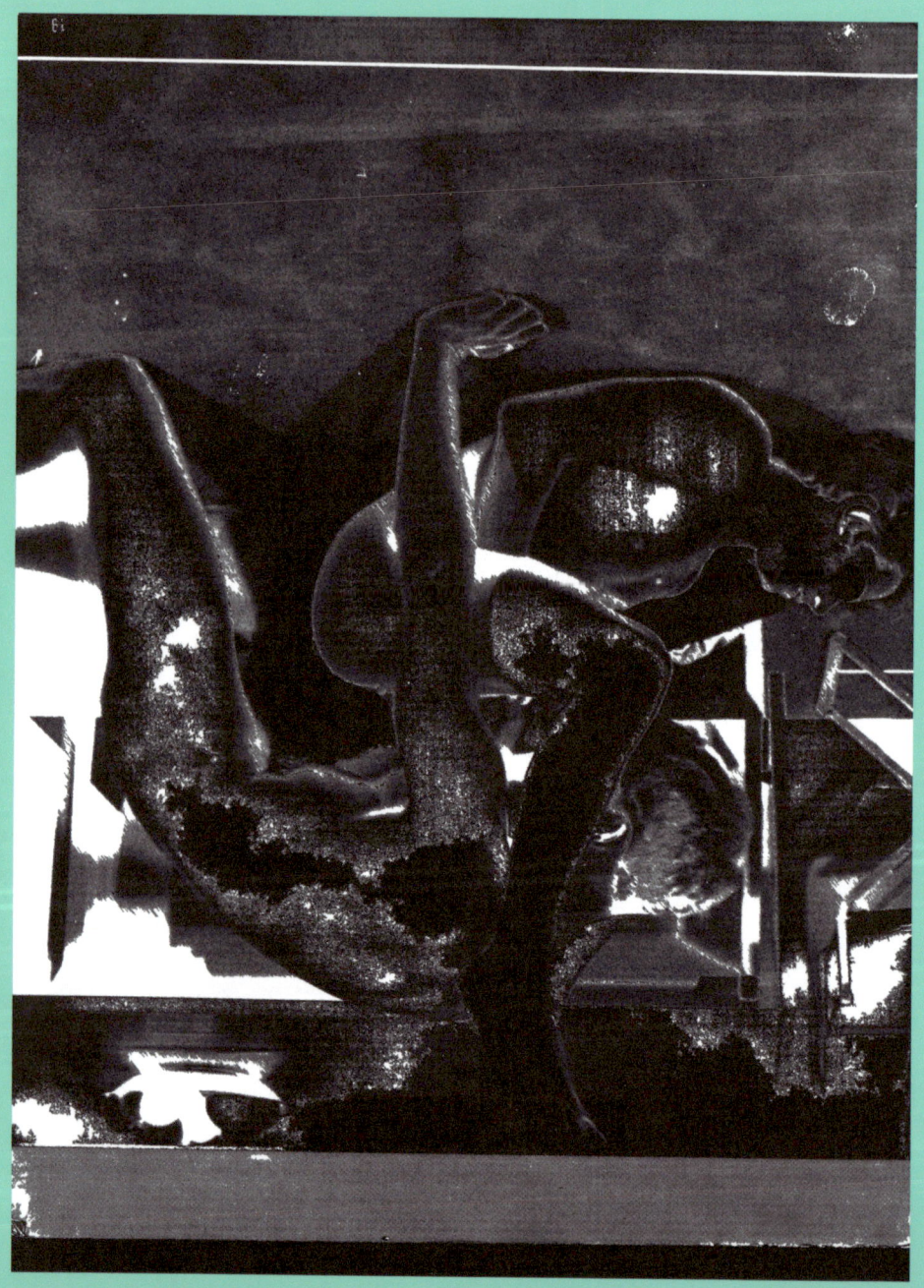

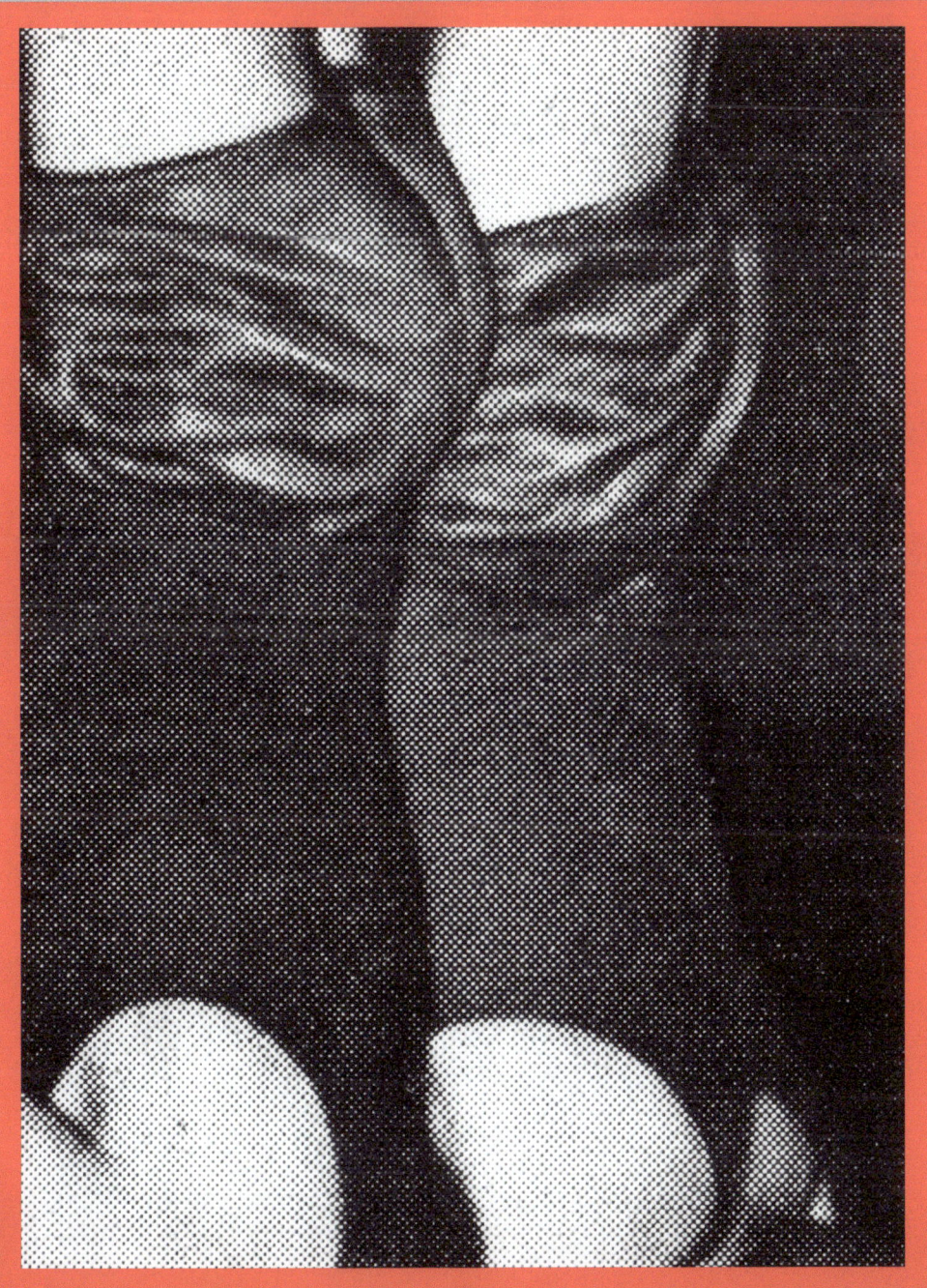

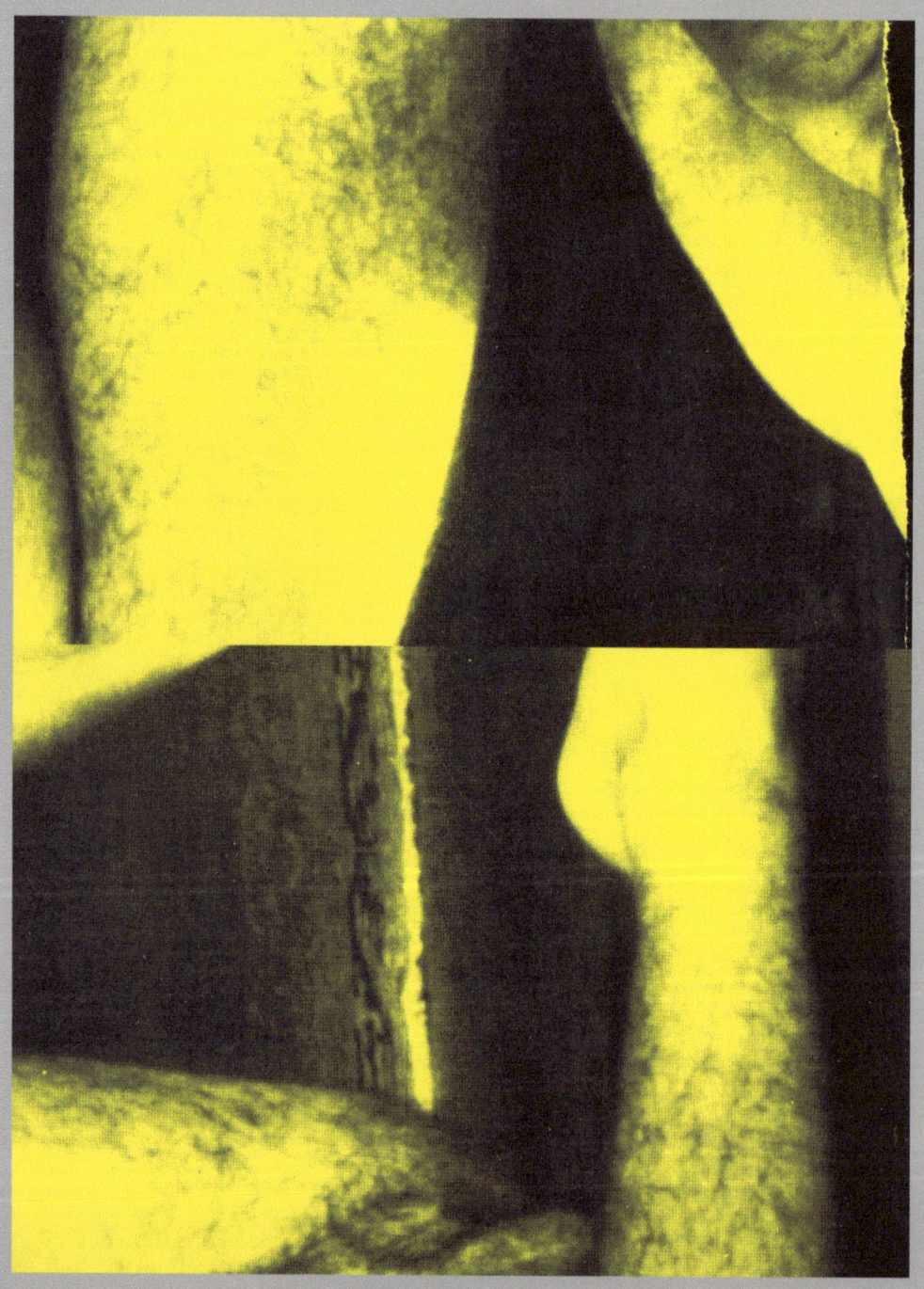

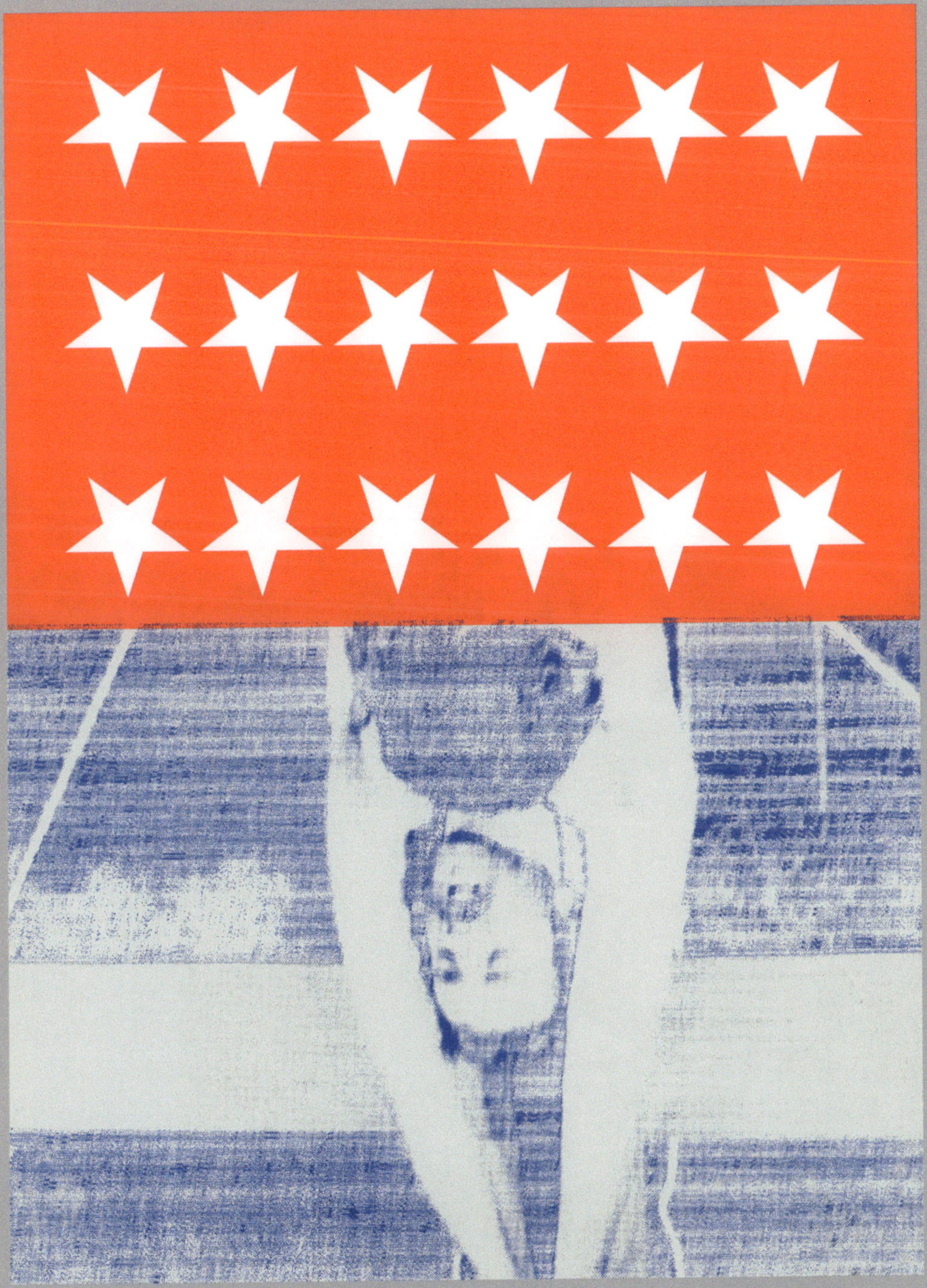

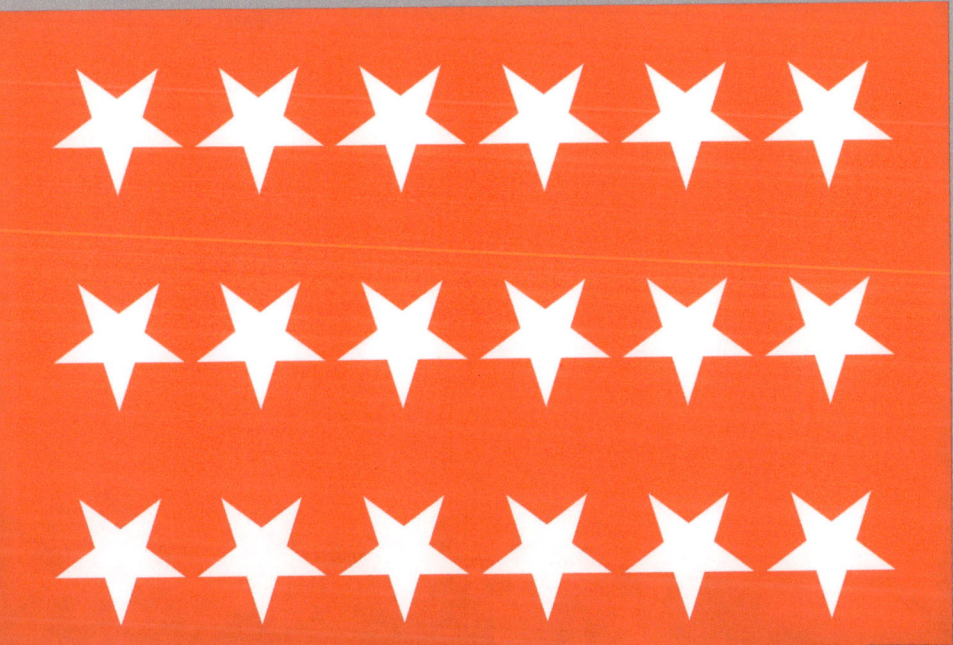

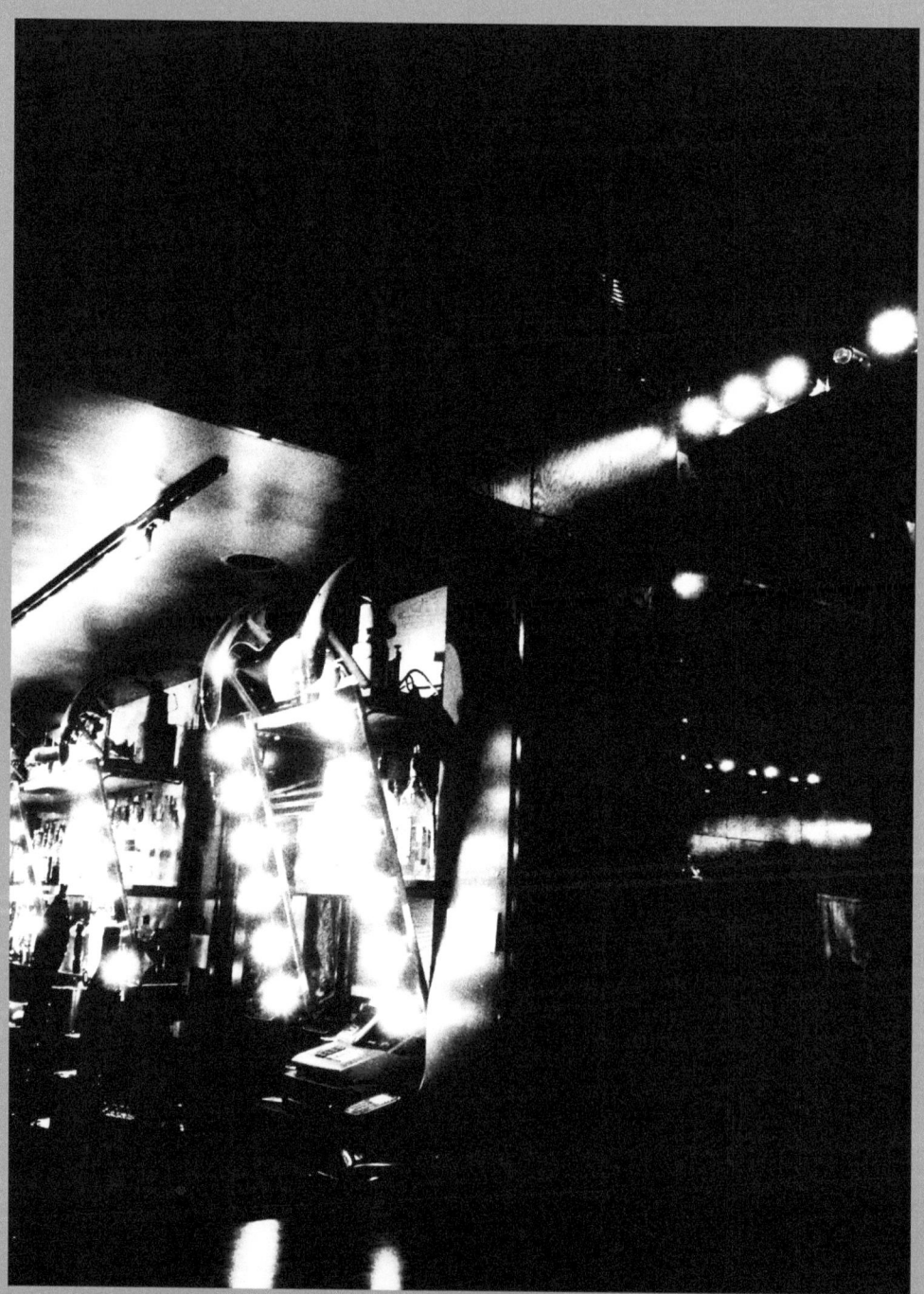

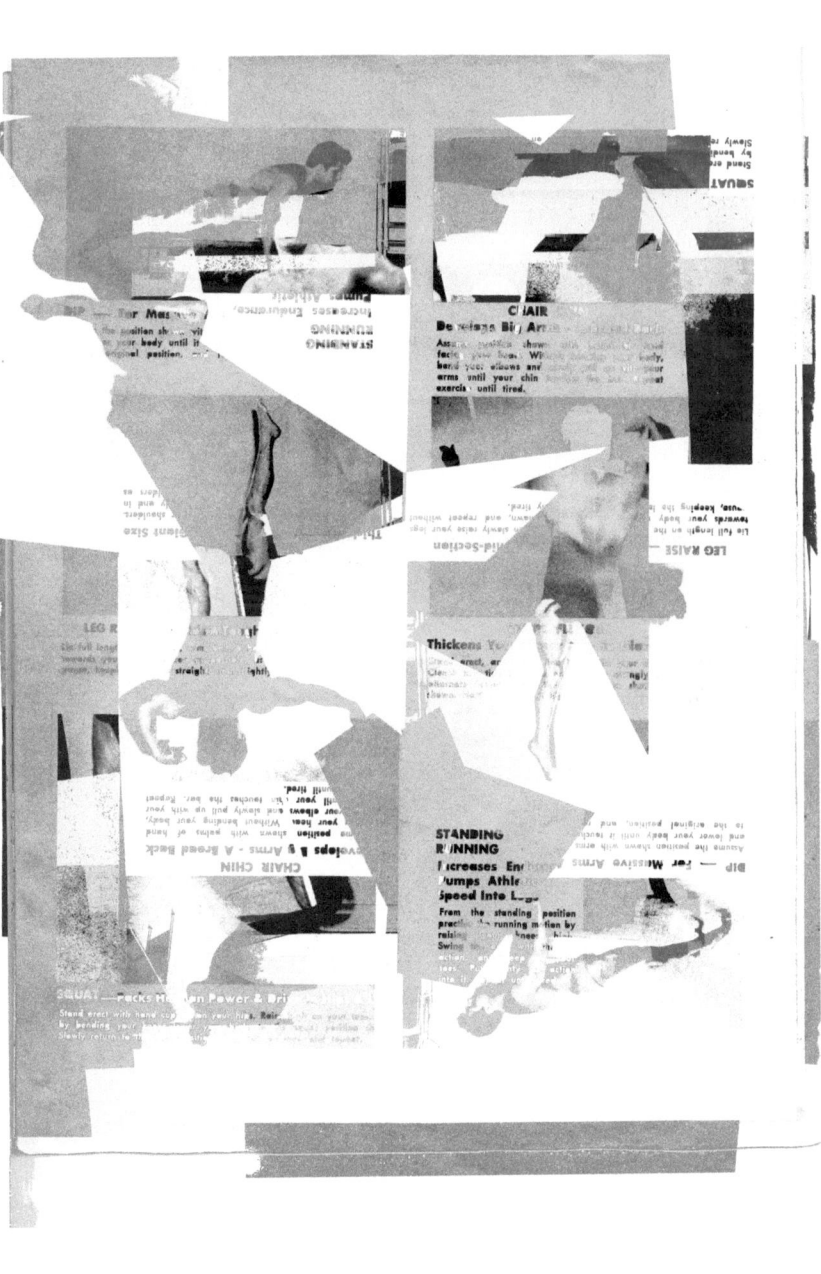

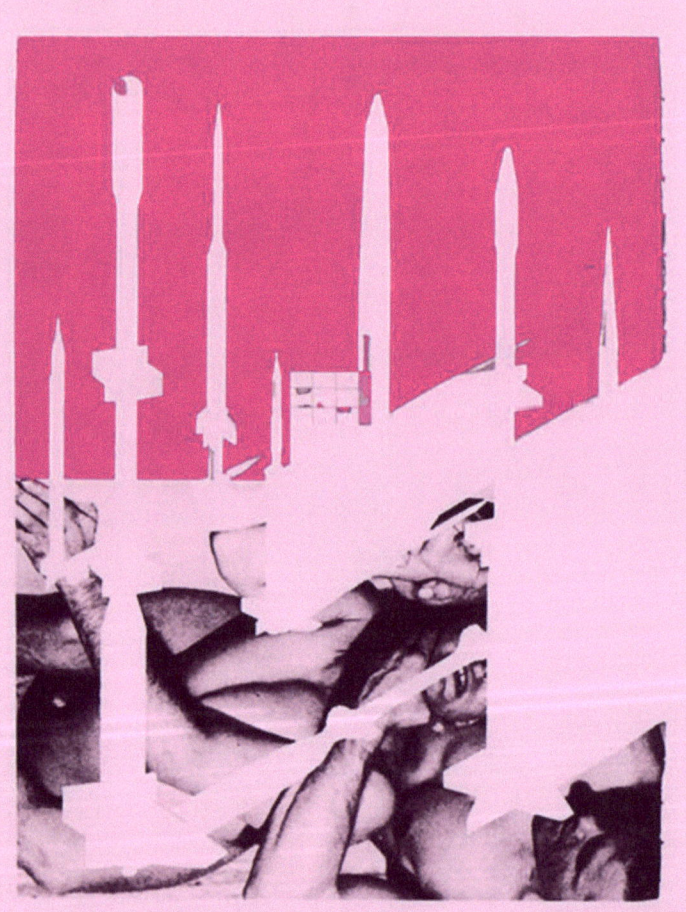

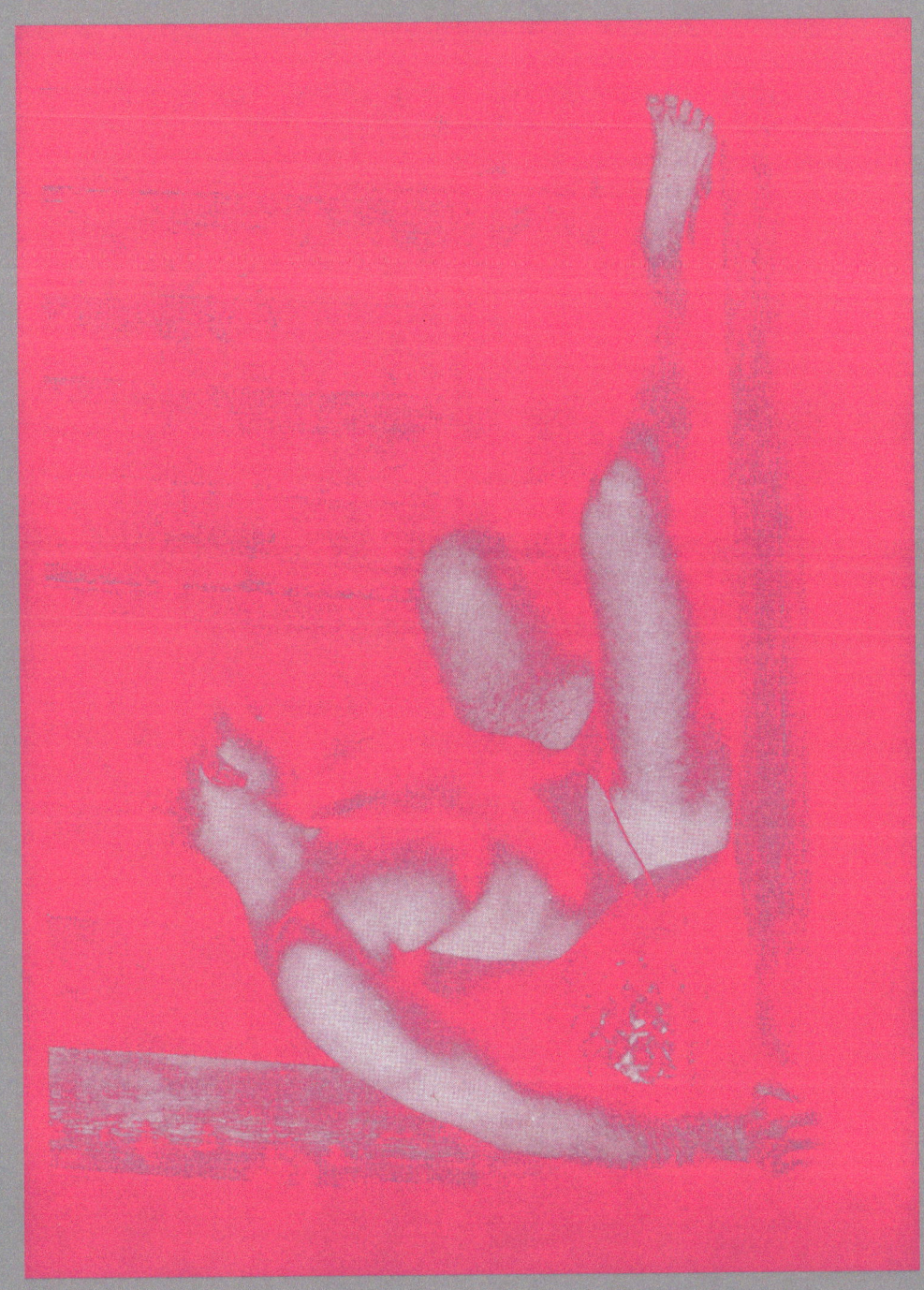

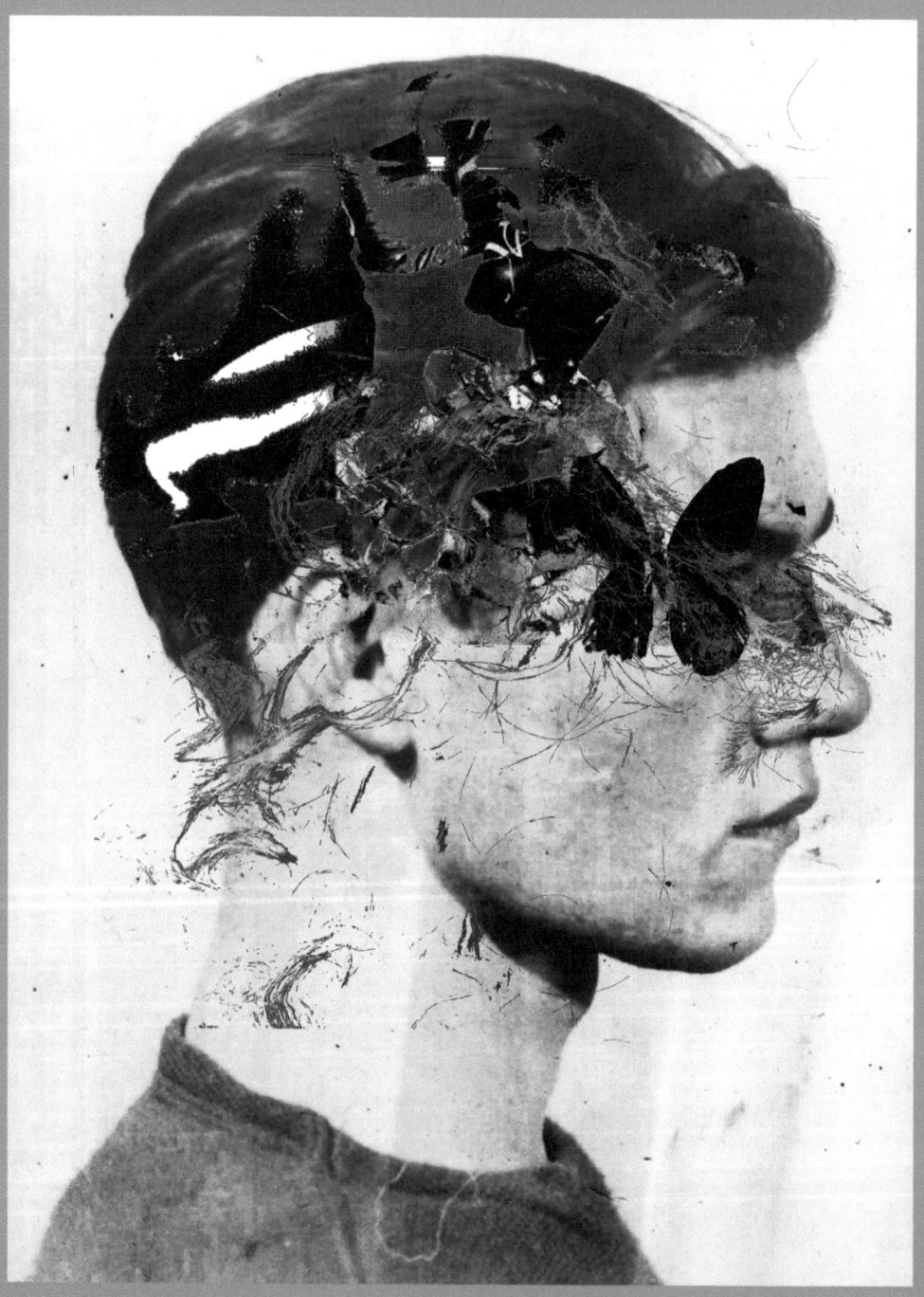

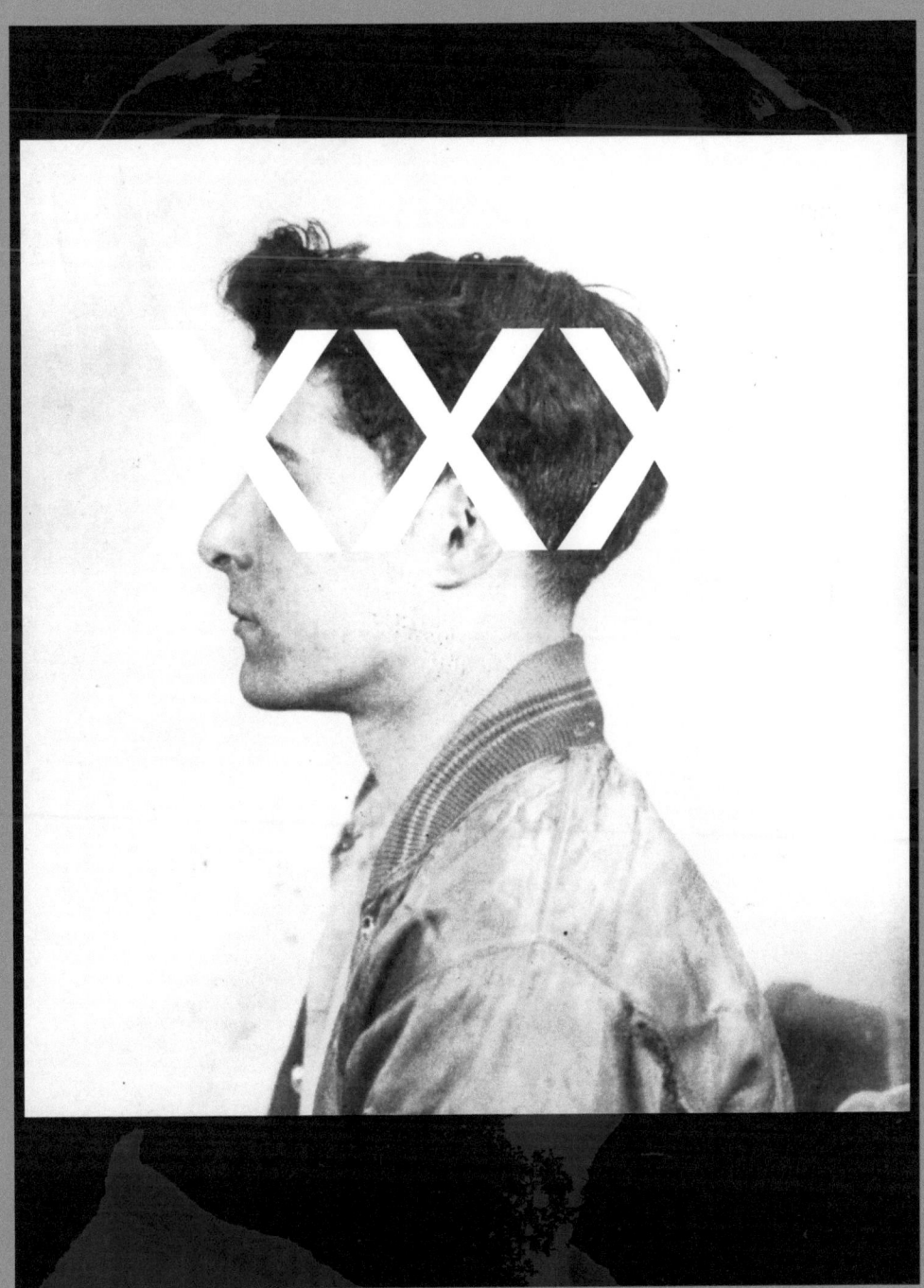

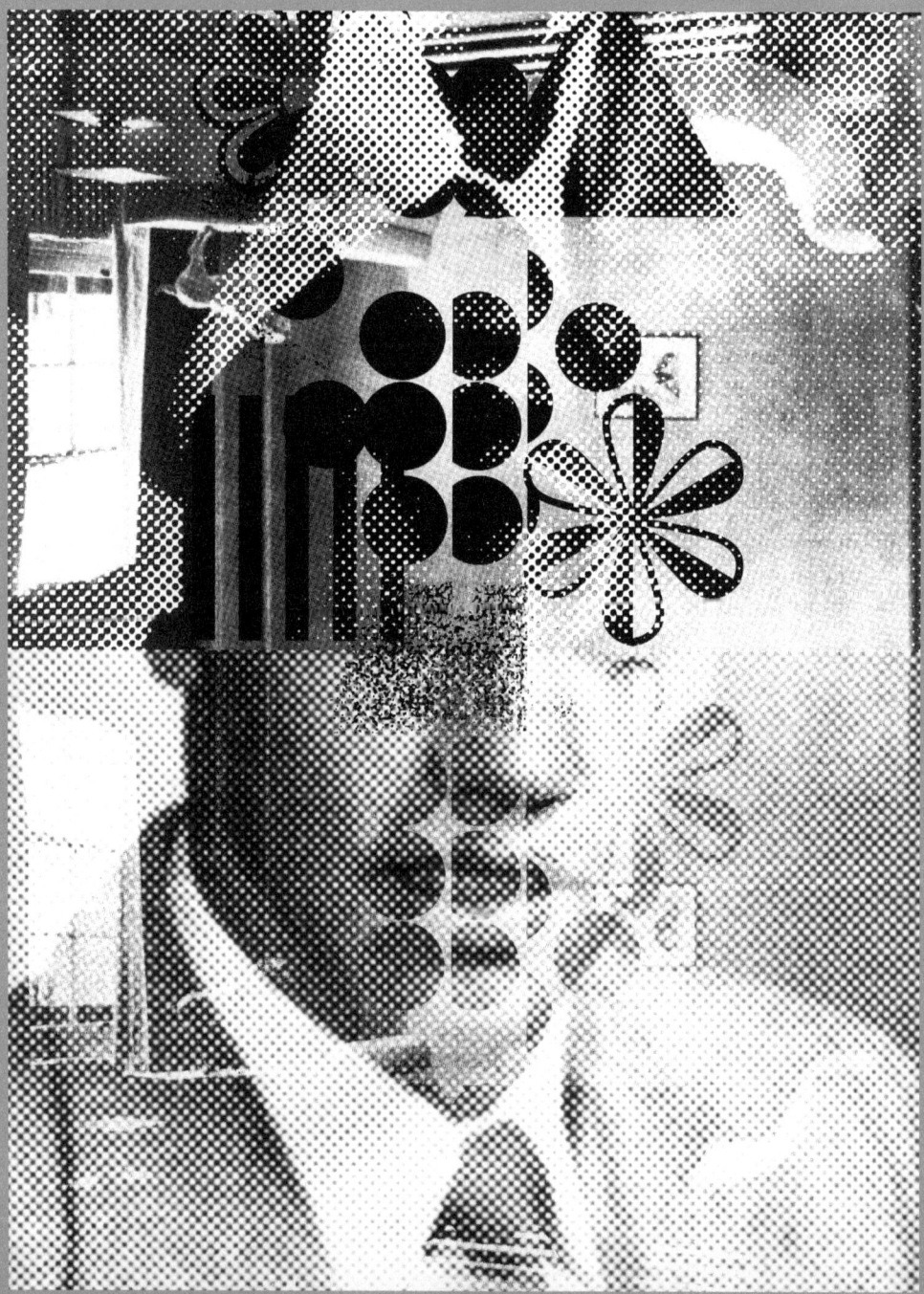

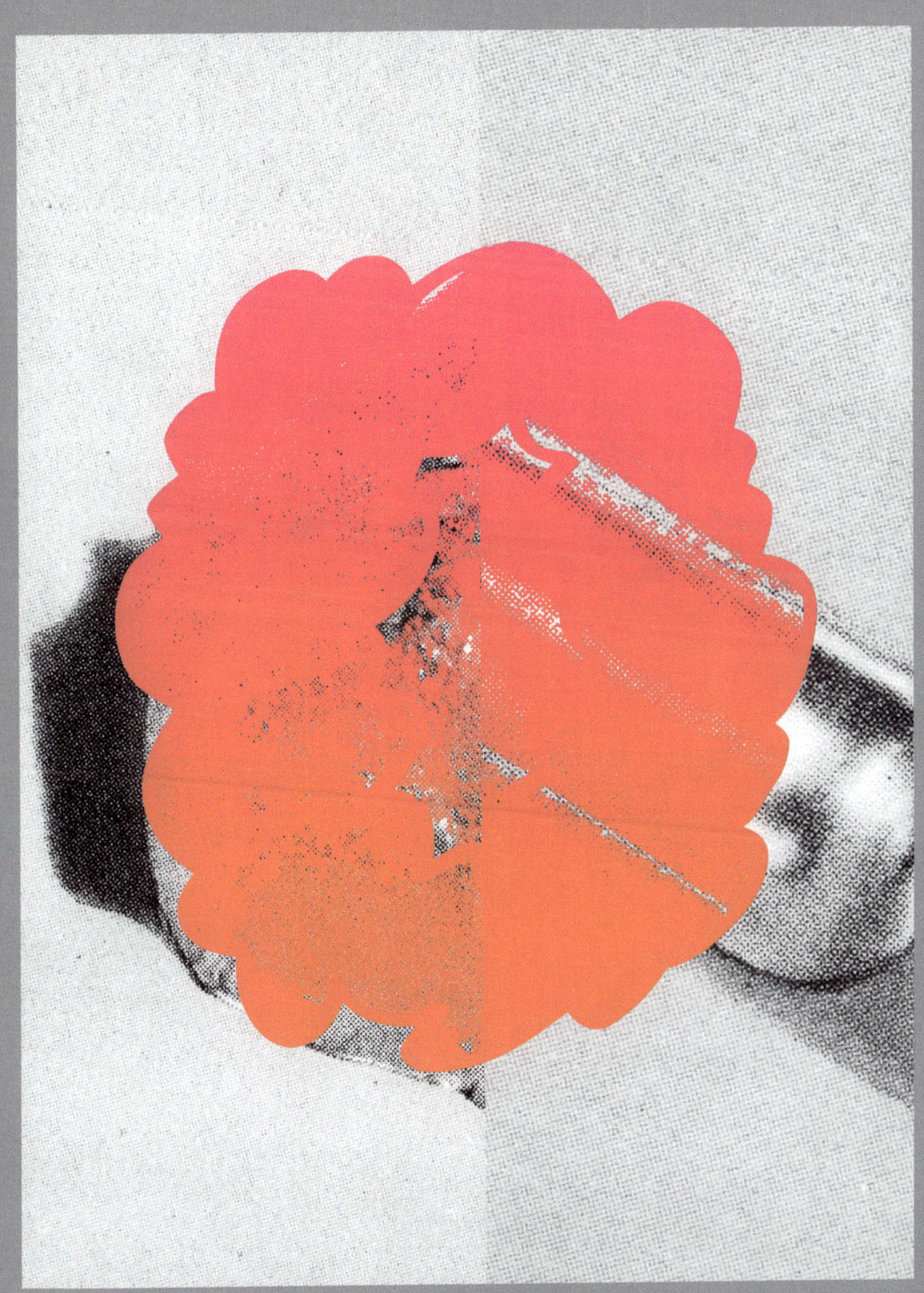

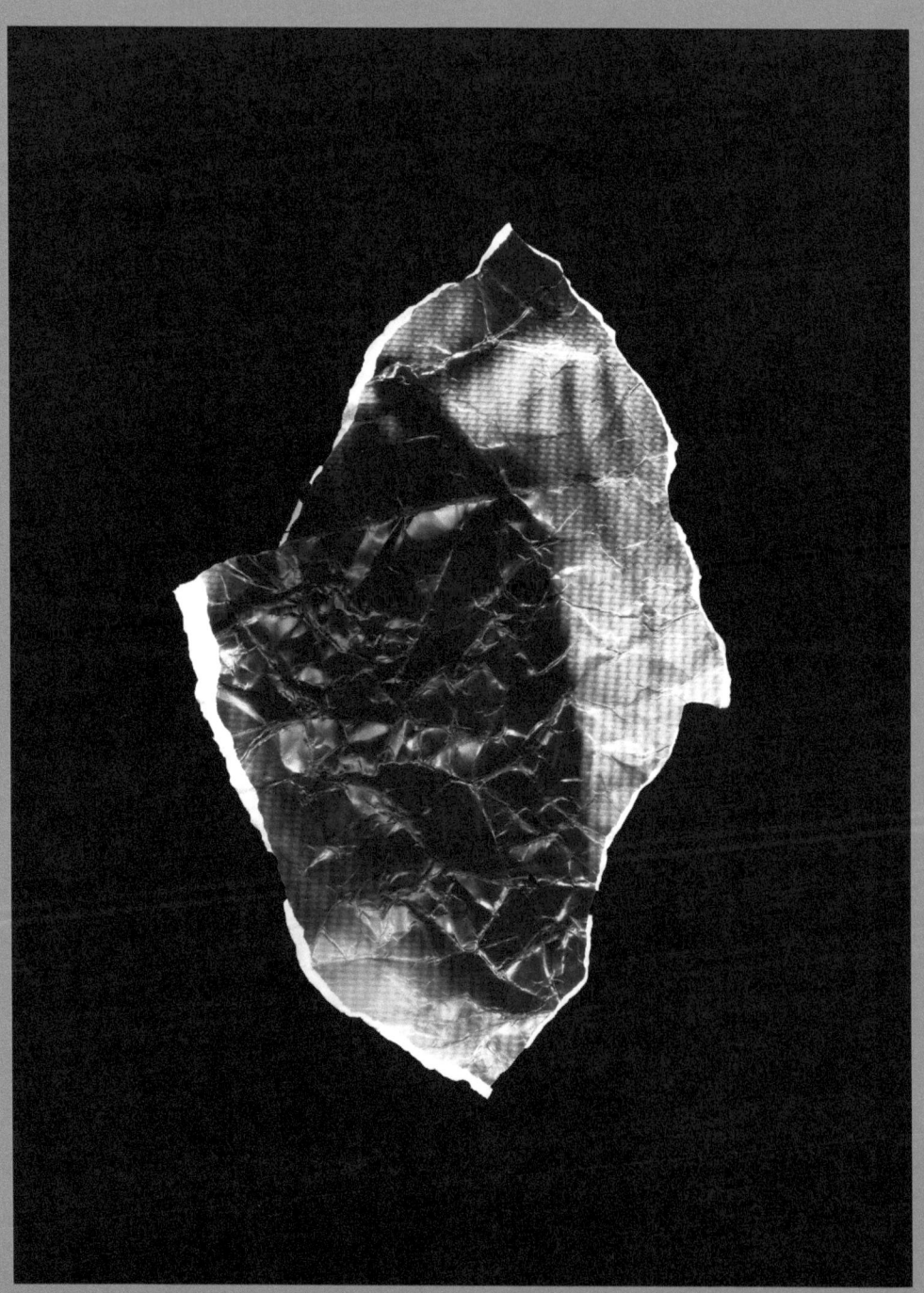

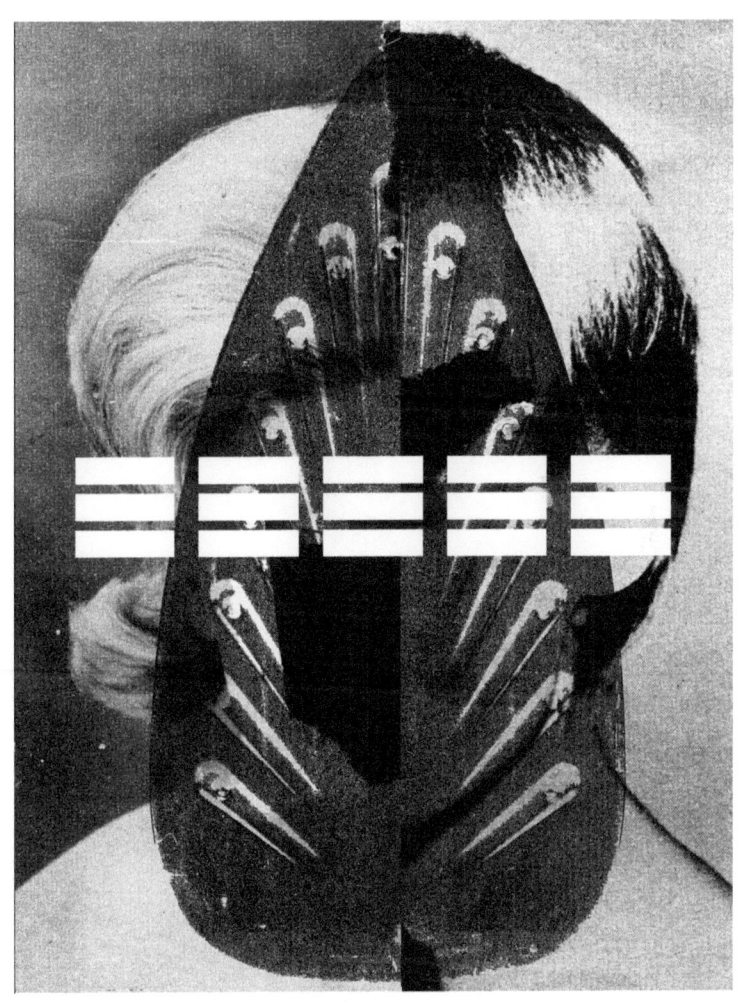

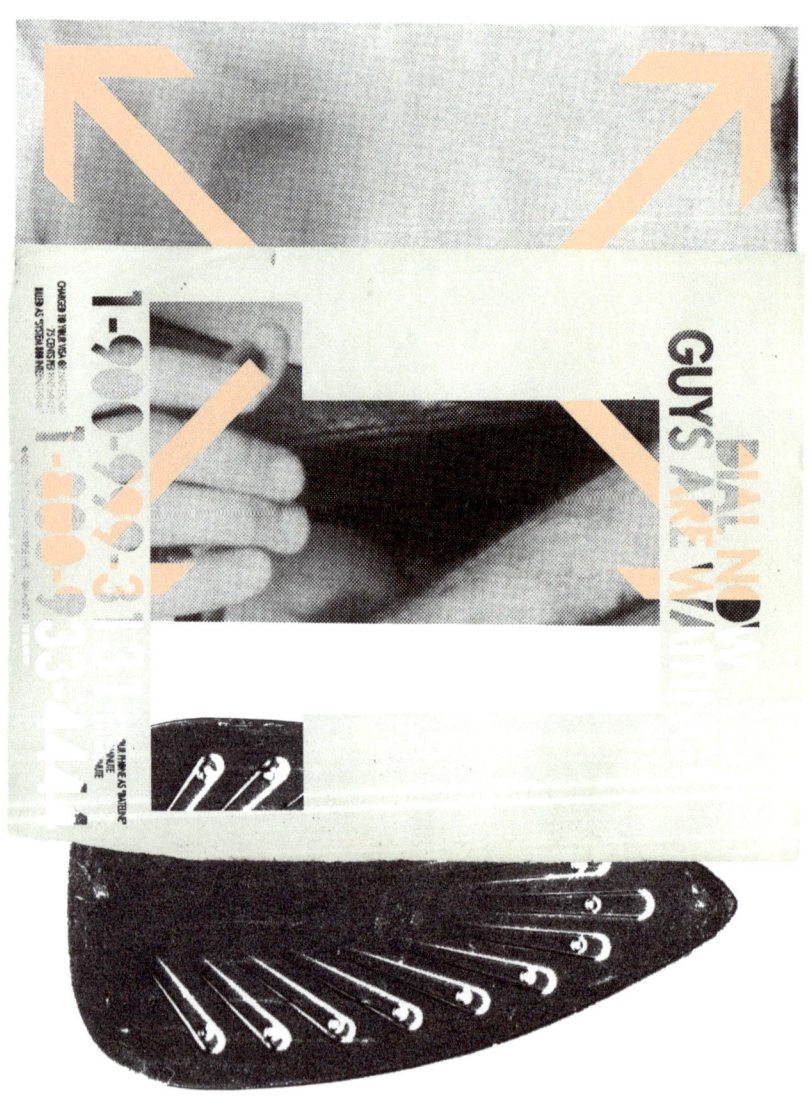

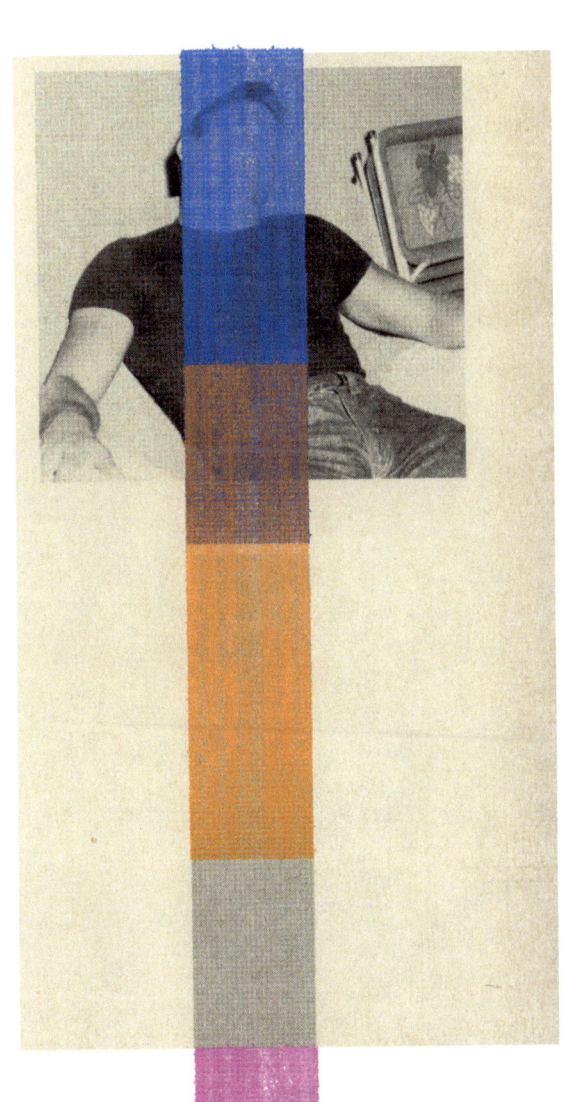

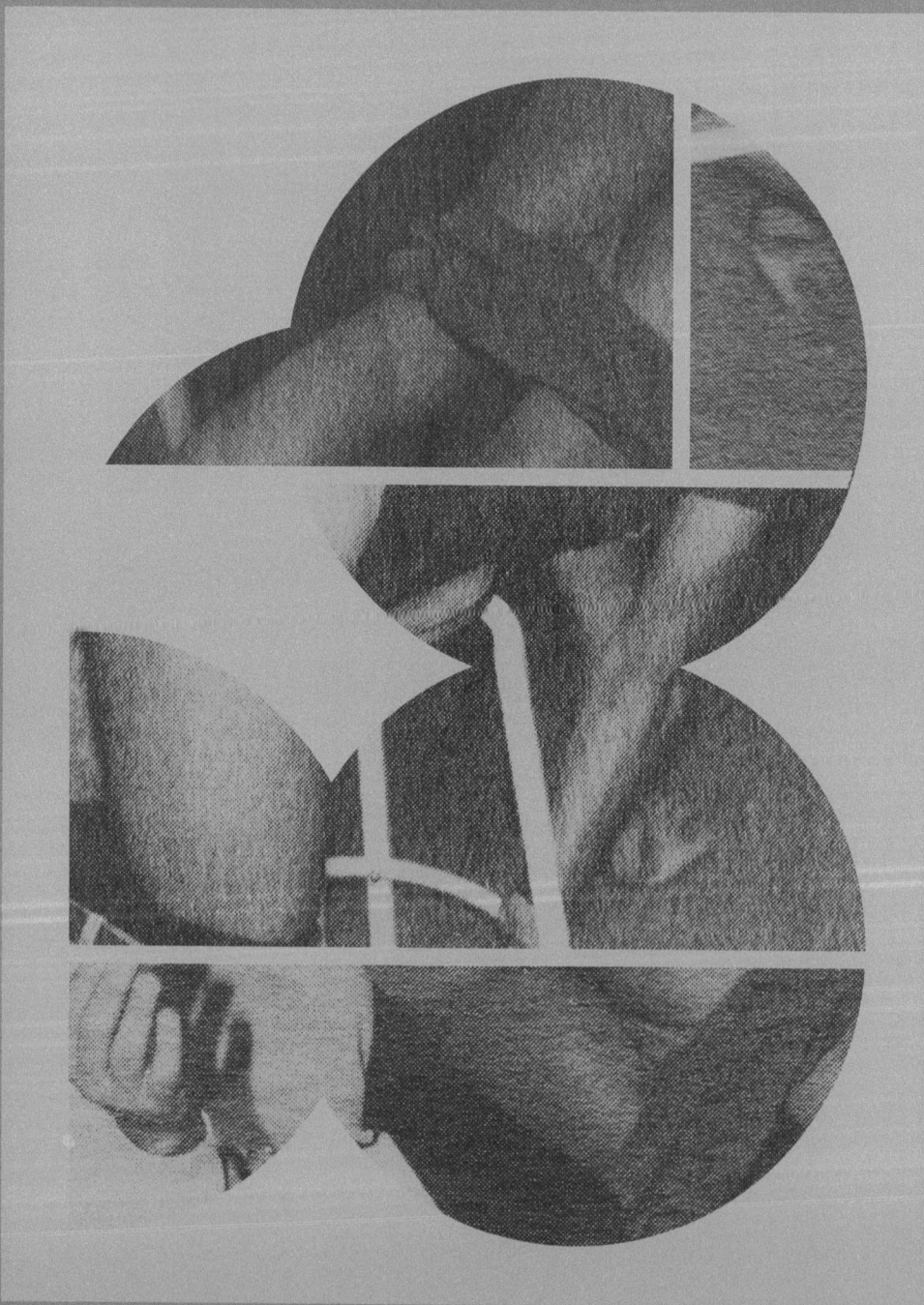

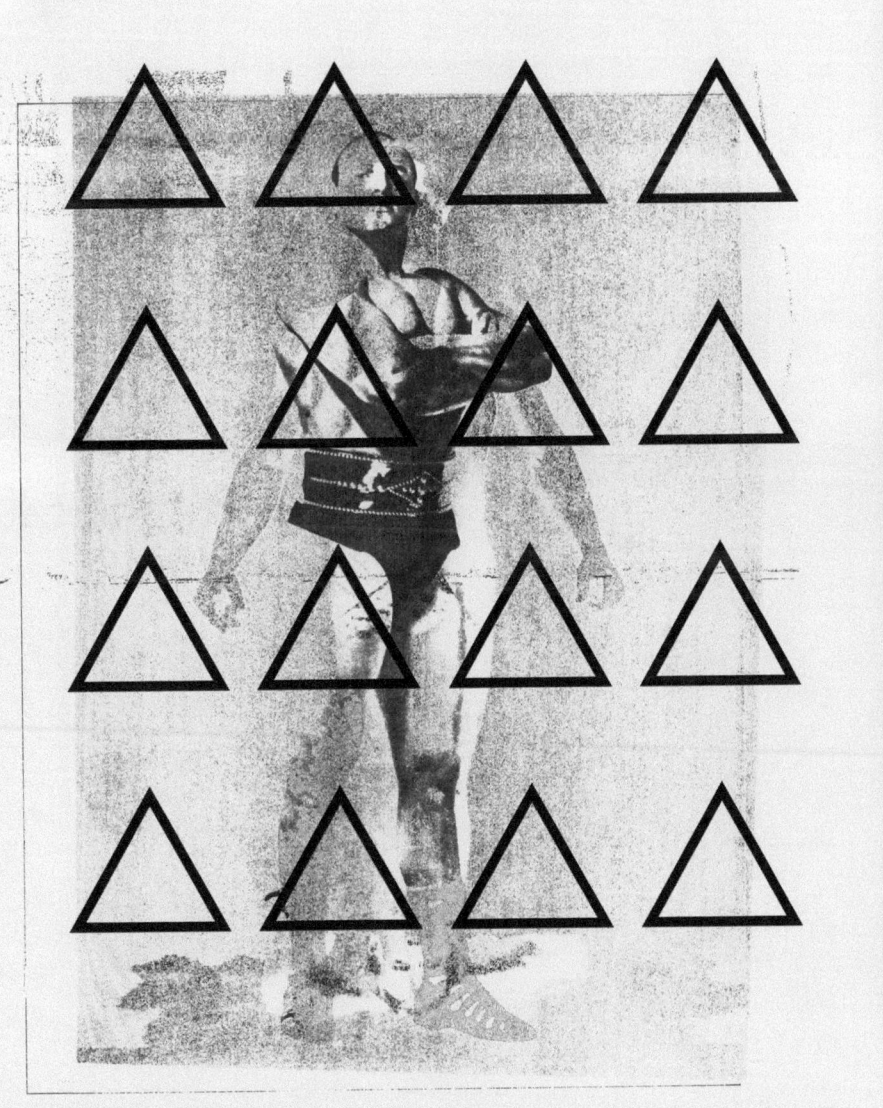

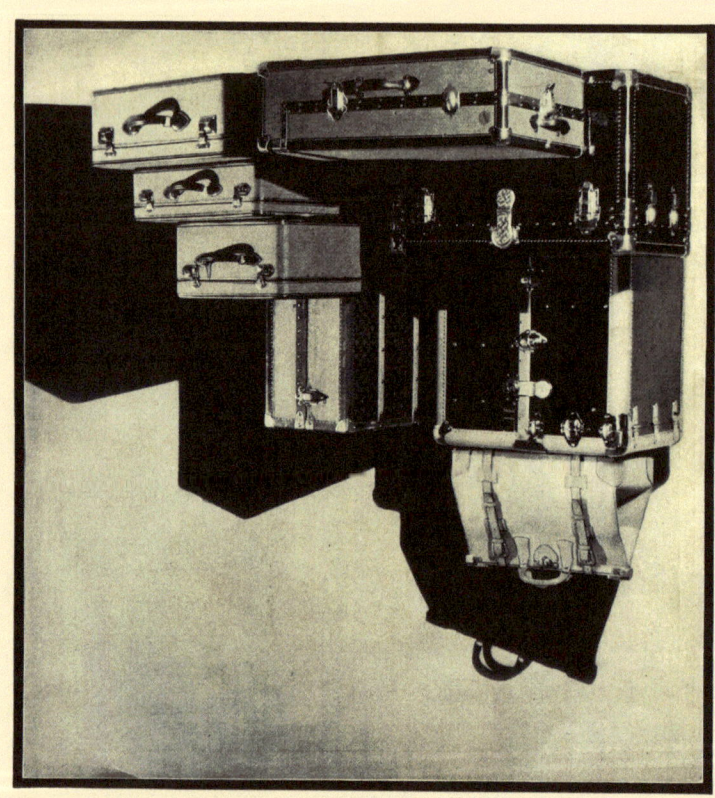

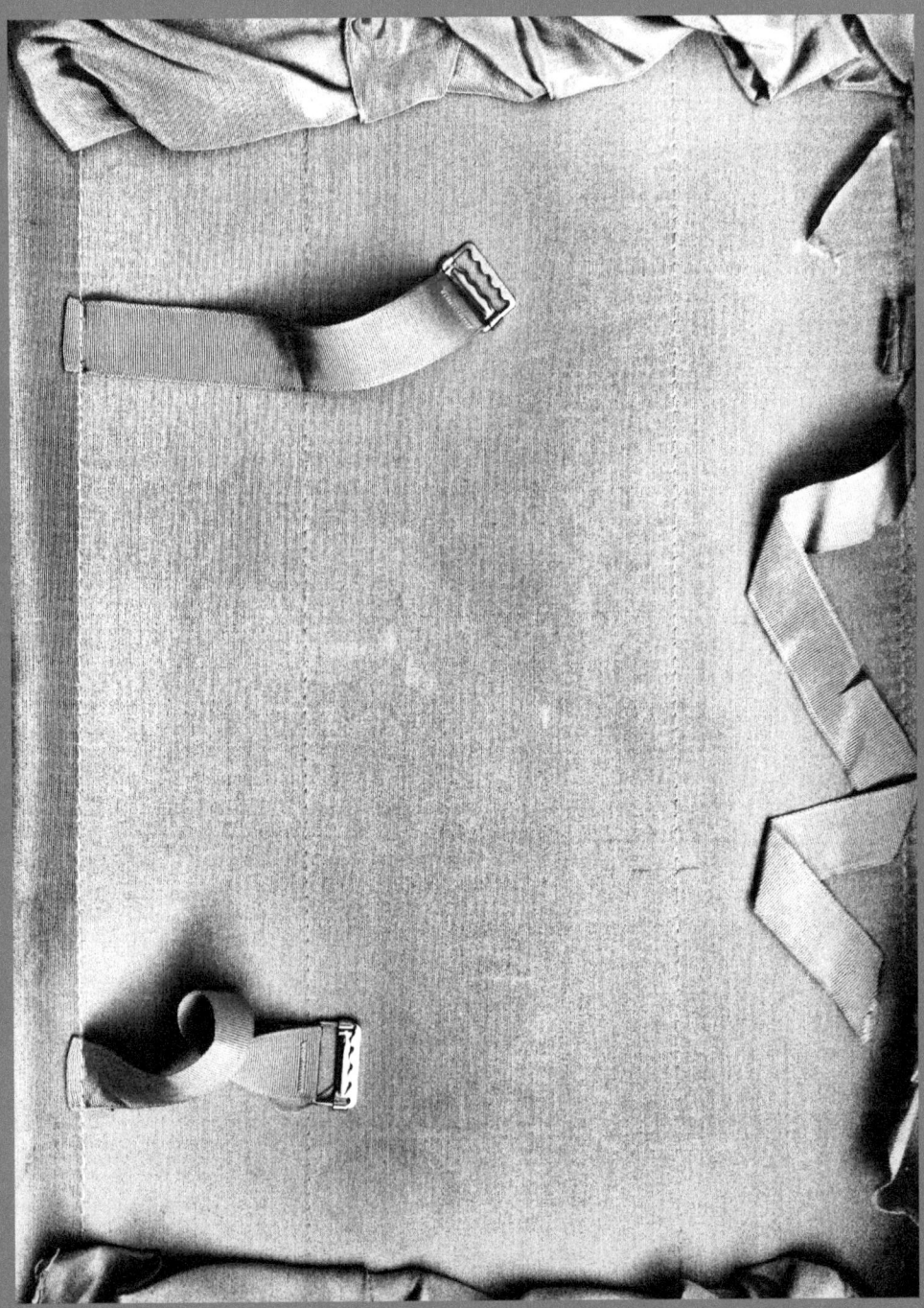

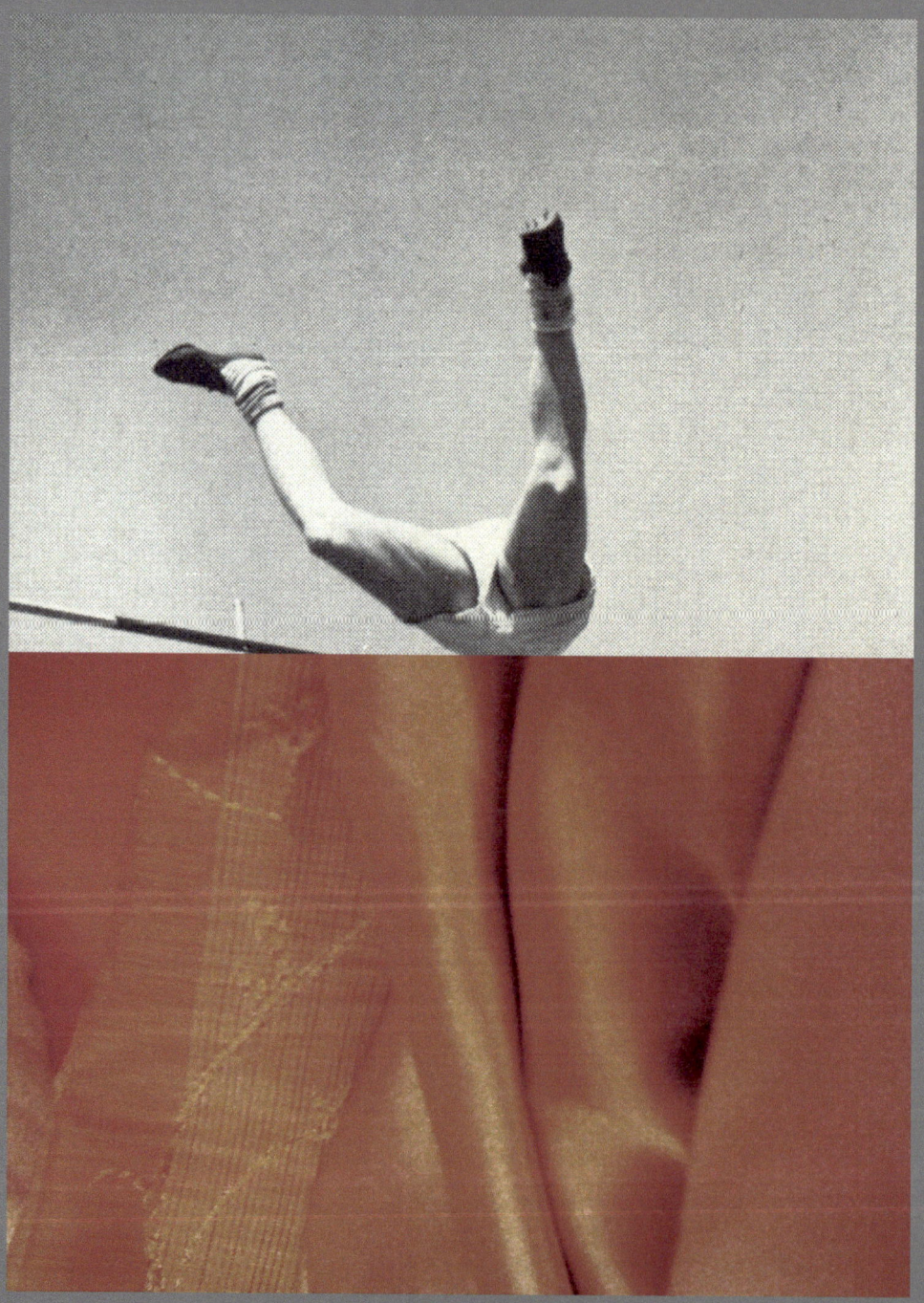

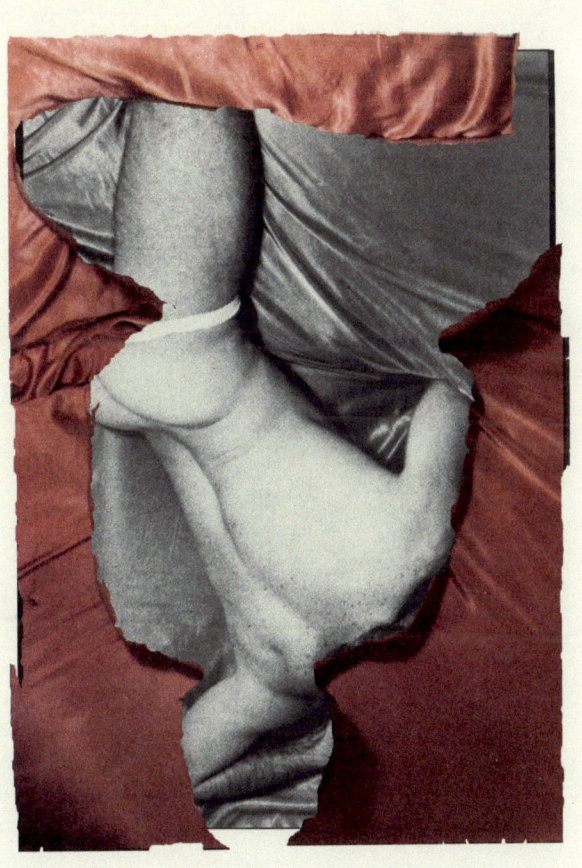

SALE

He gathers 'em up one way or another,

as the Dungec
ncept and a

------

5); ■ SLAVES FO
■VHS.
ok (9.95)
Charge my ■VISA
Exp. Date._____

_____
_____
_____
_____

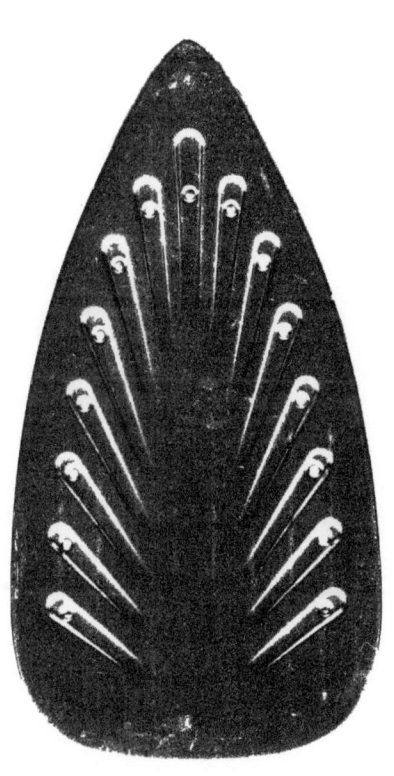

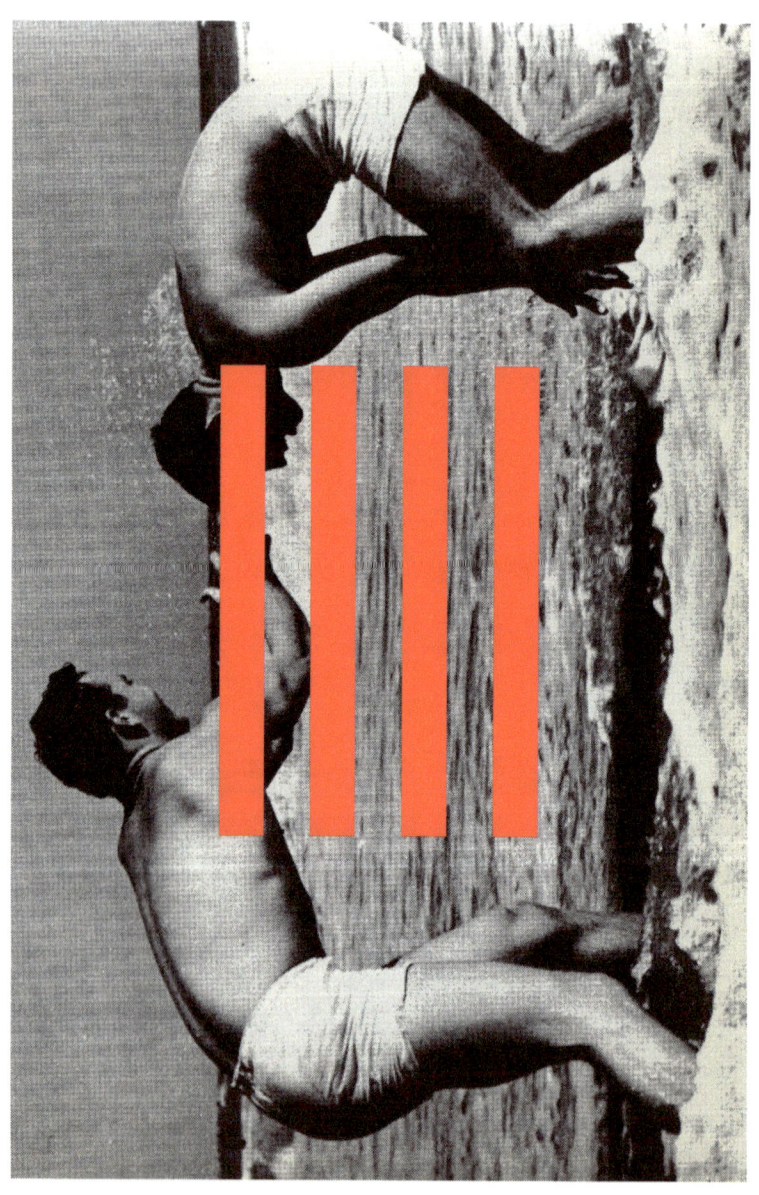

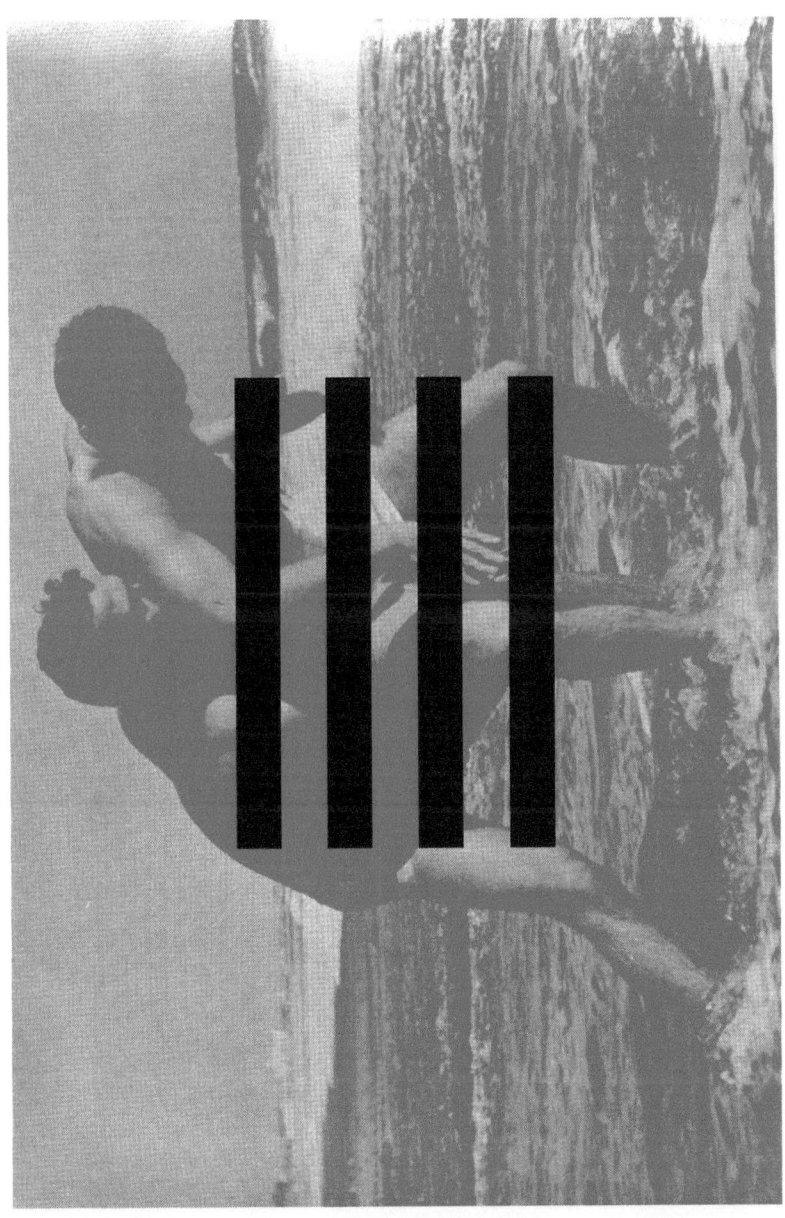

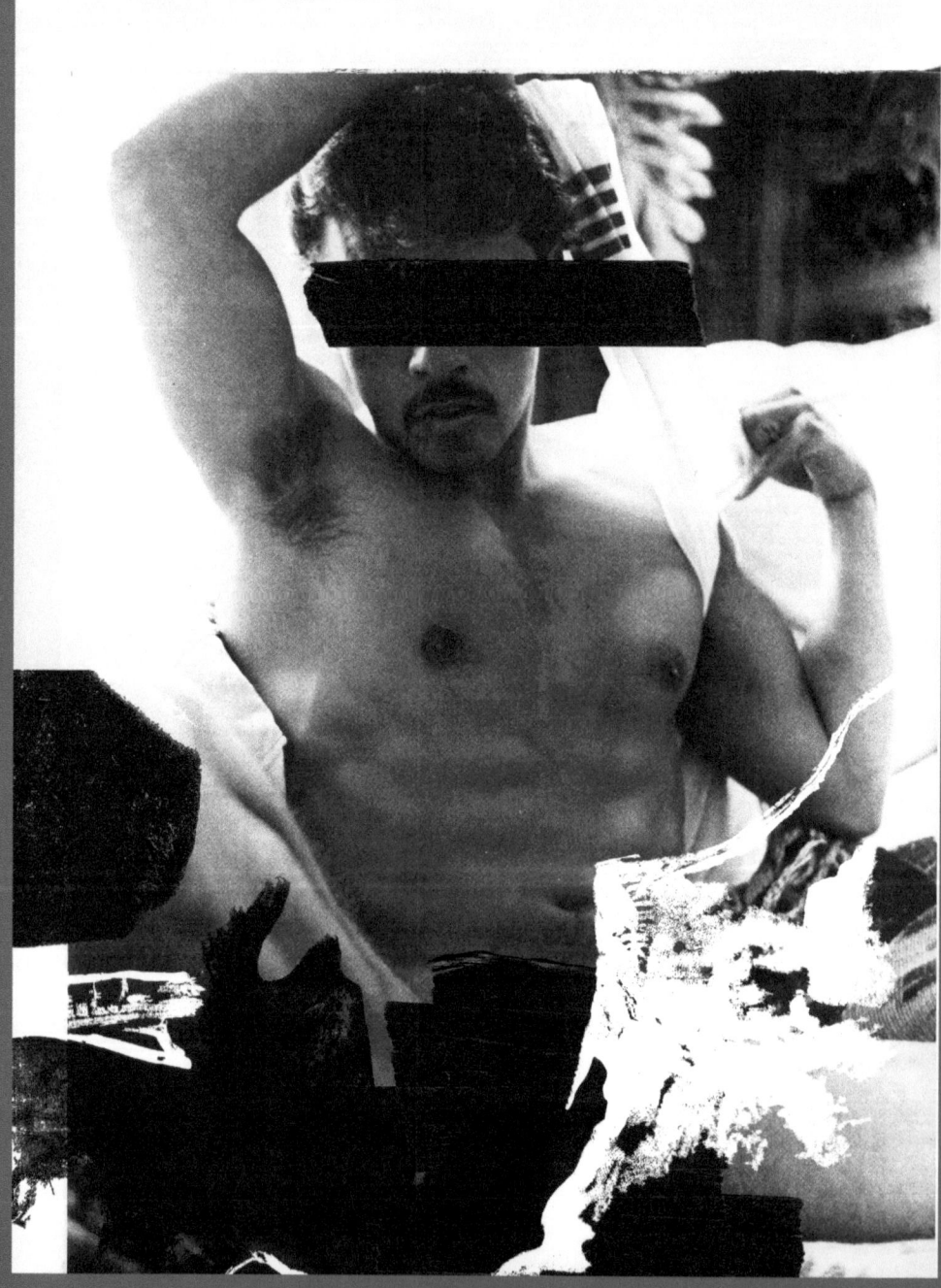

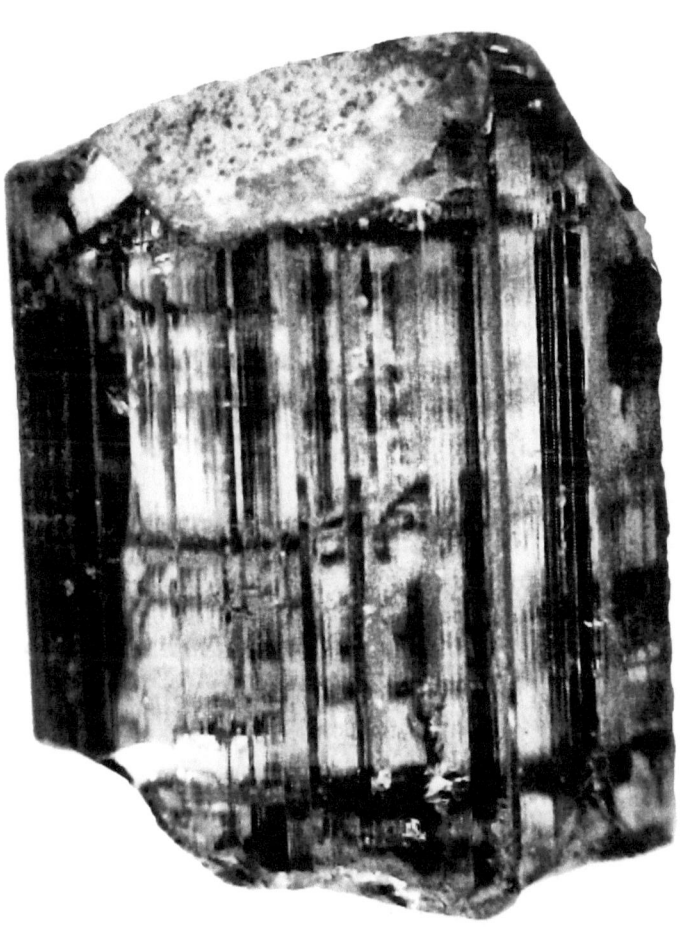

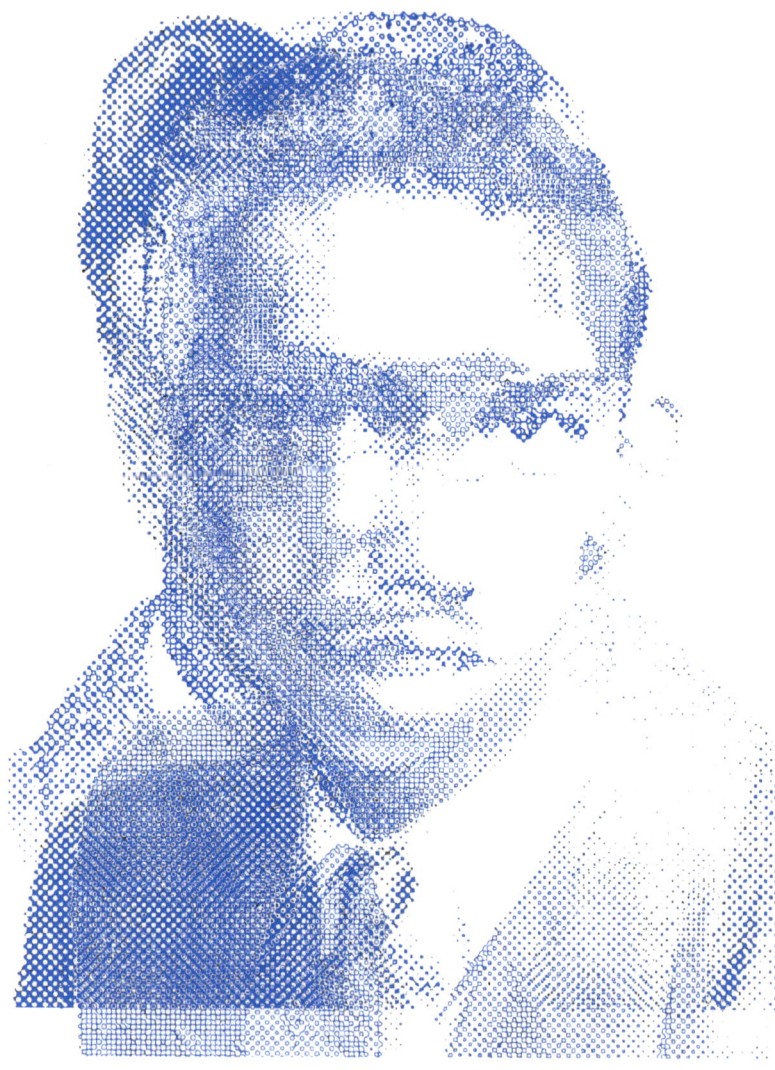

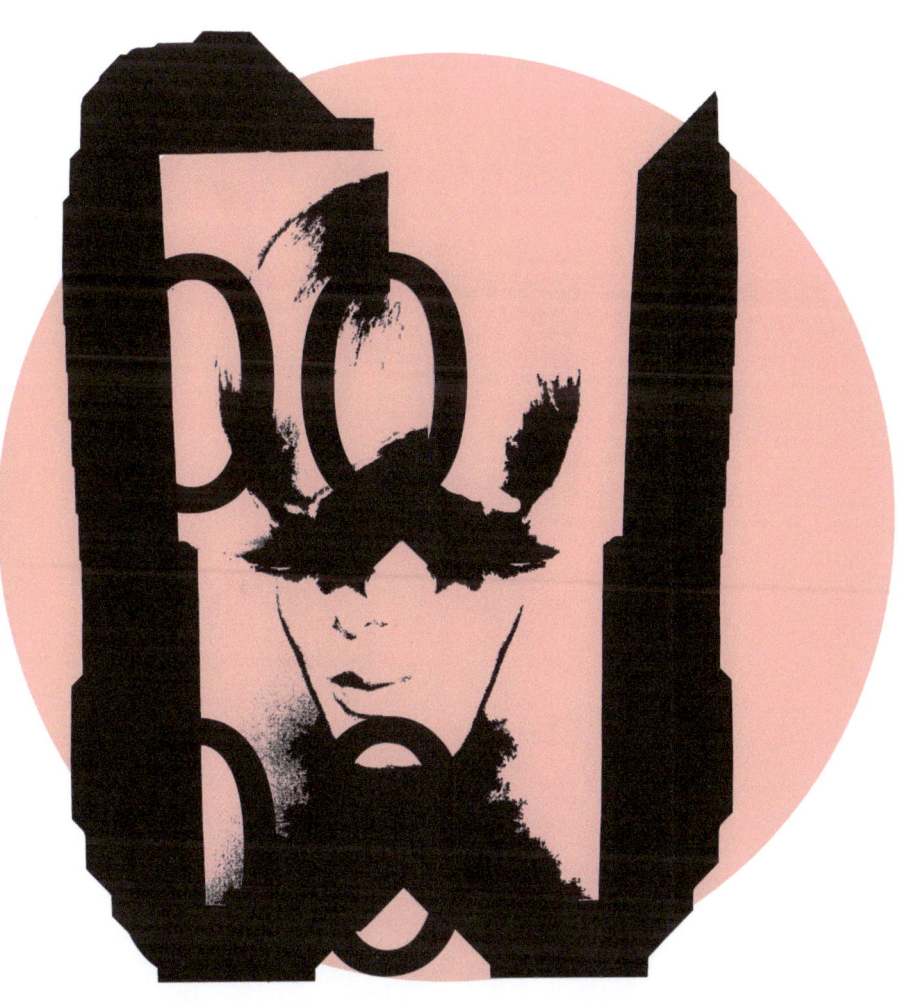

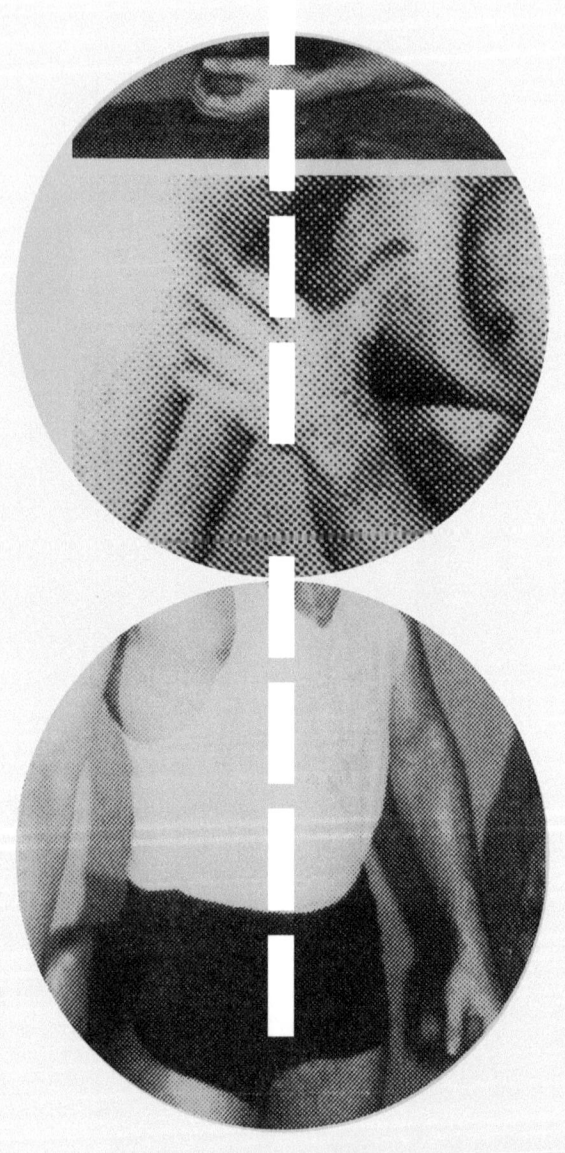

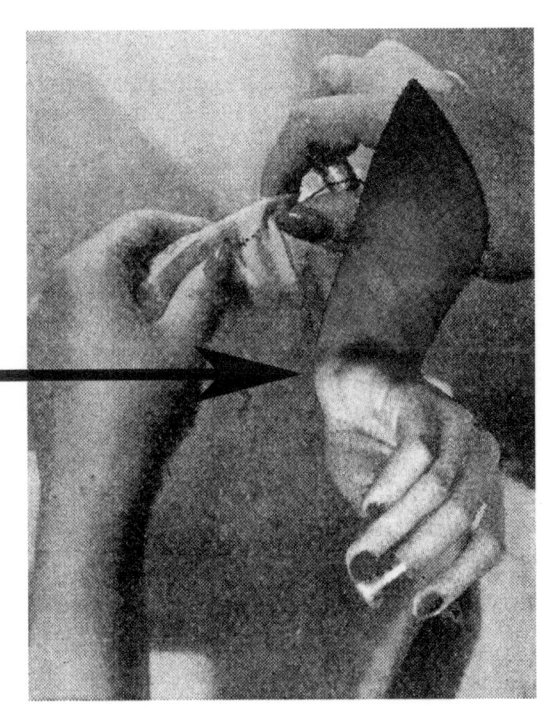

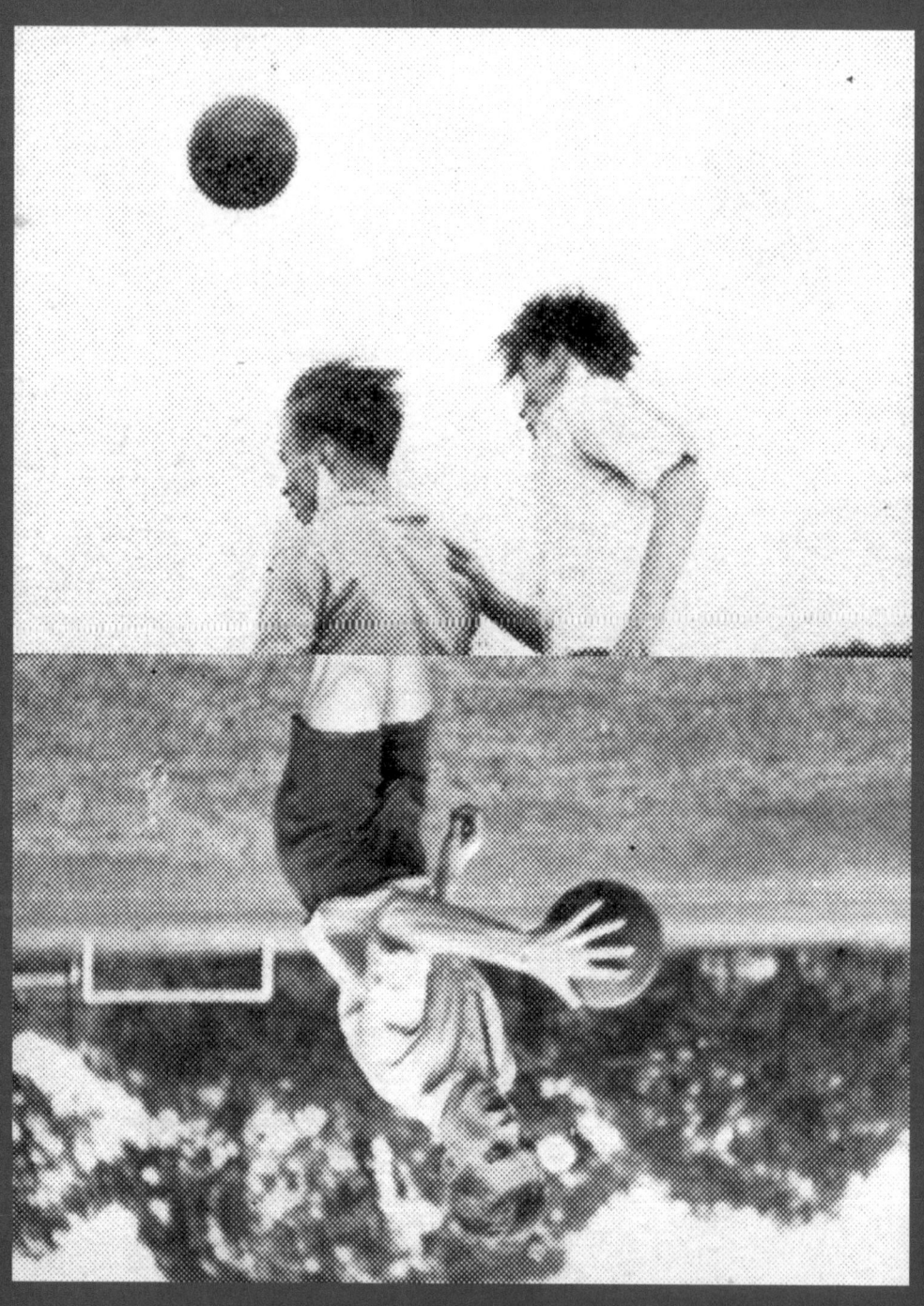

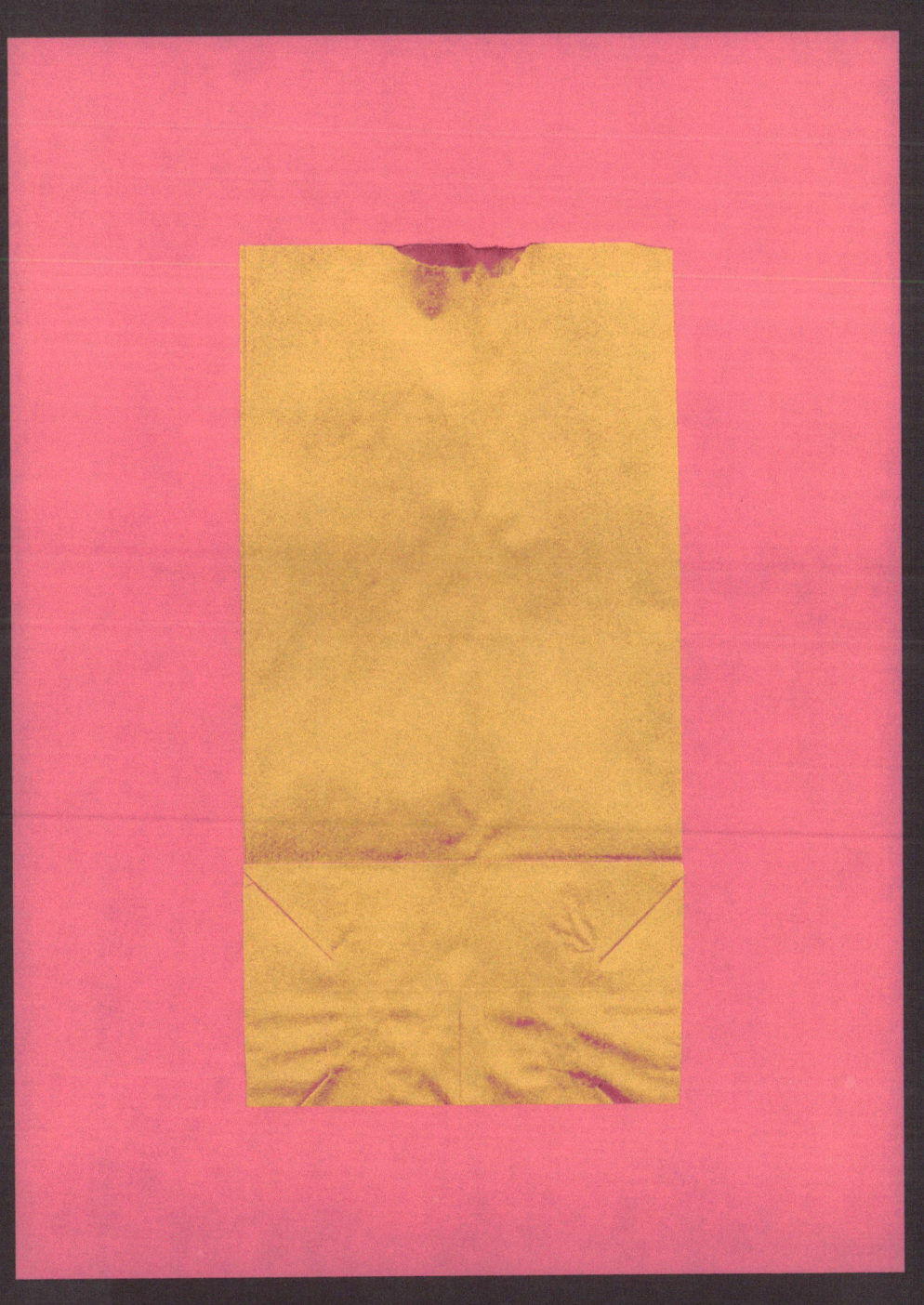

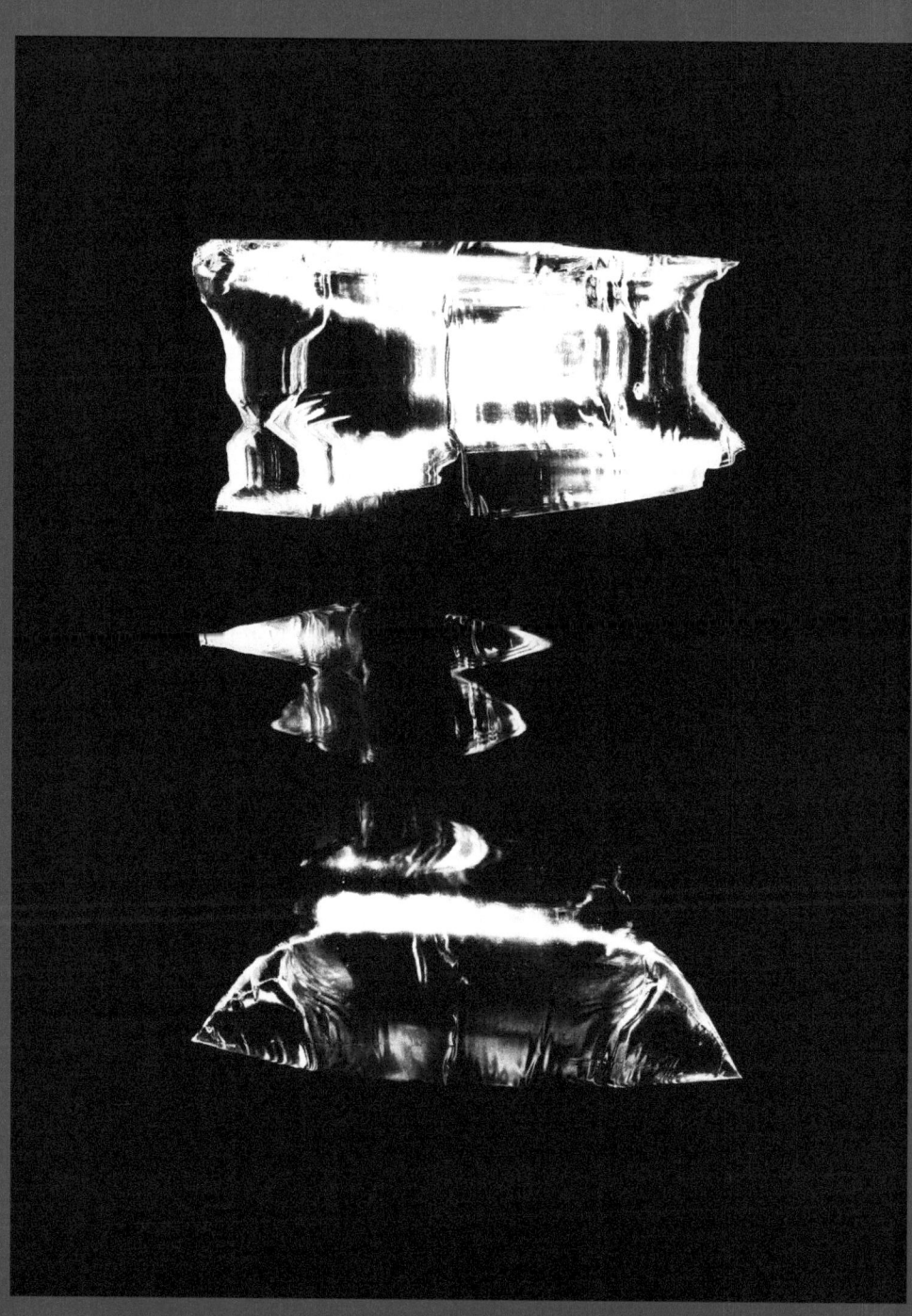

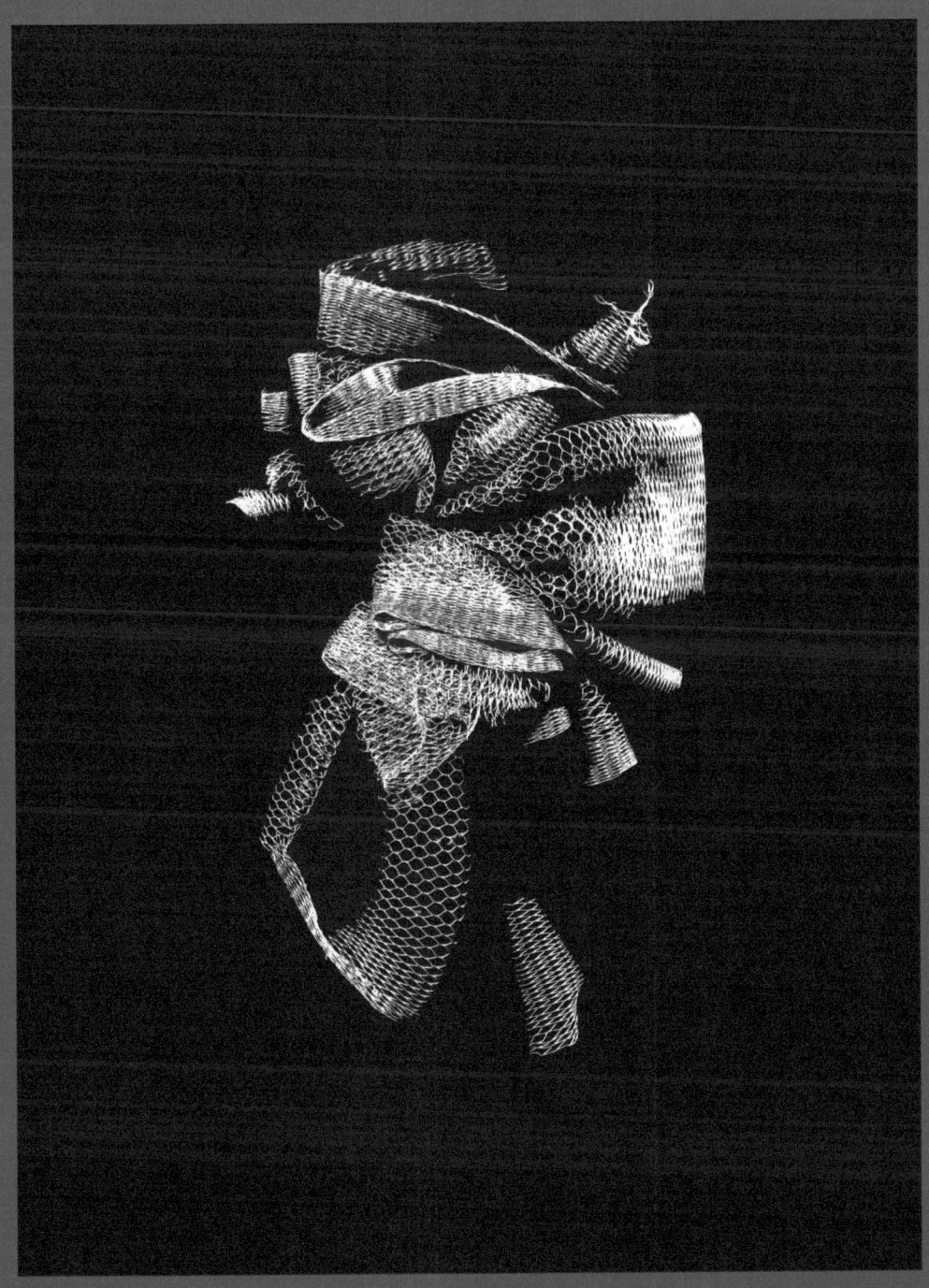

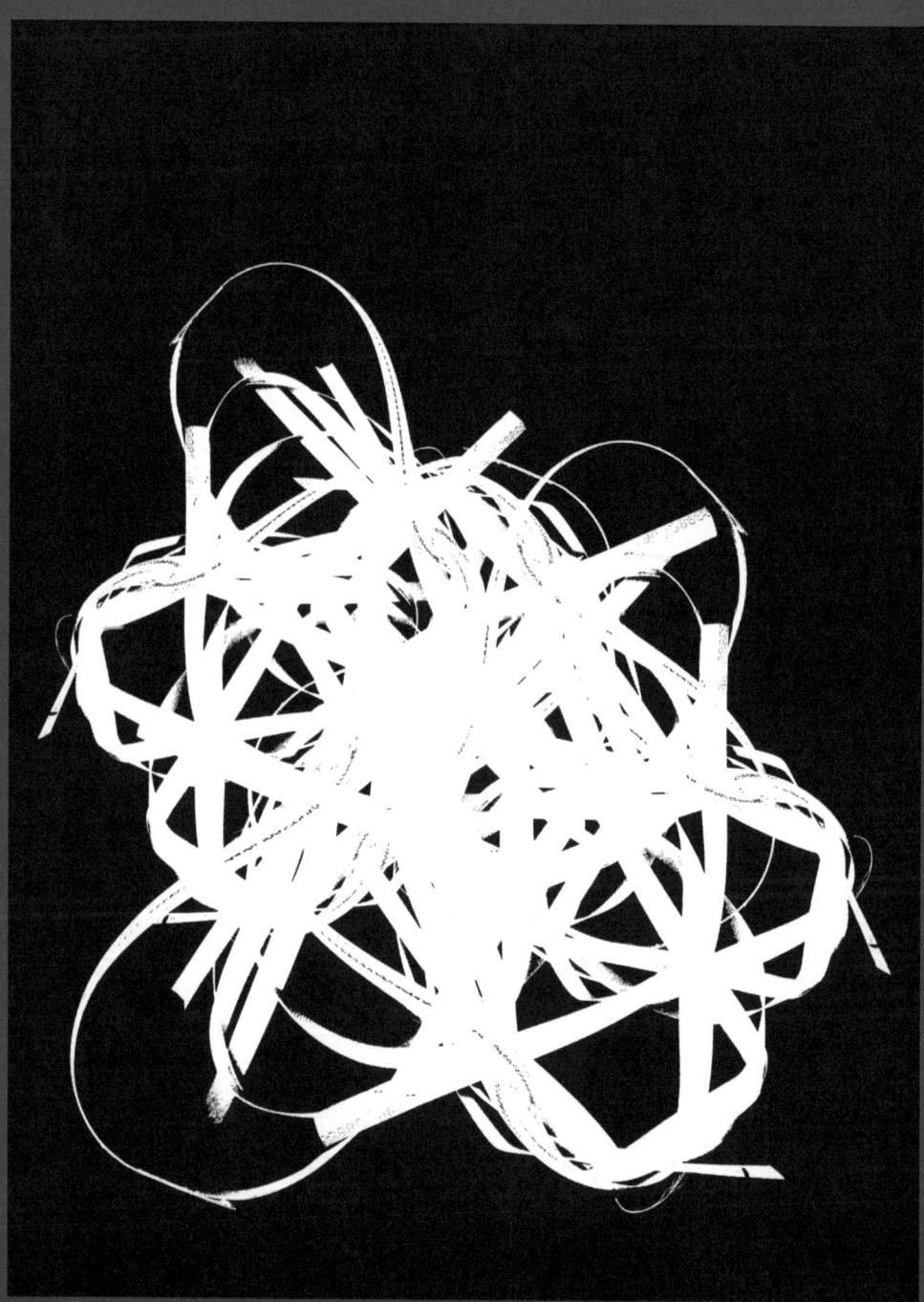

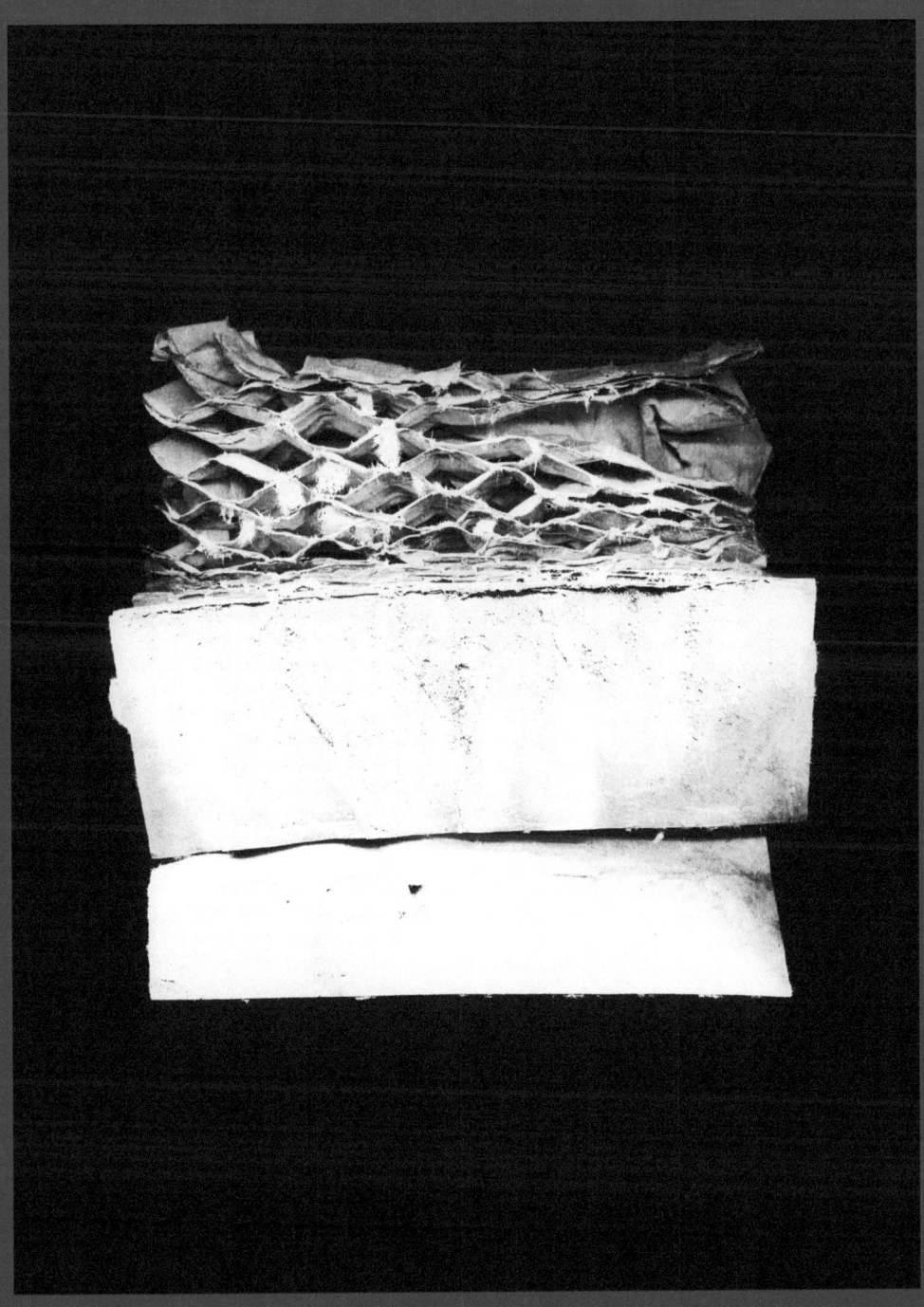

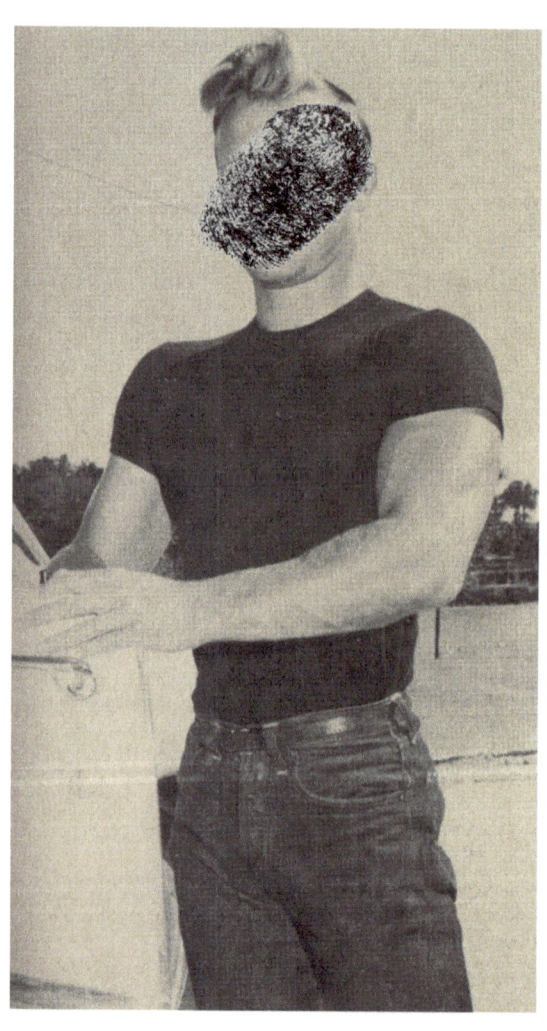

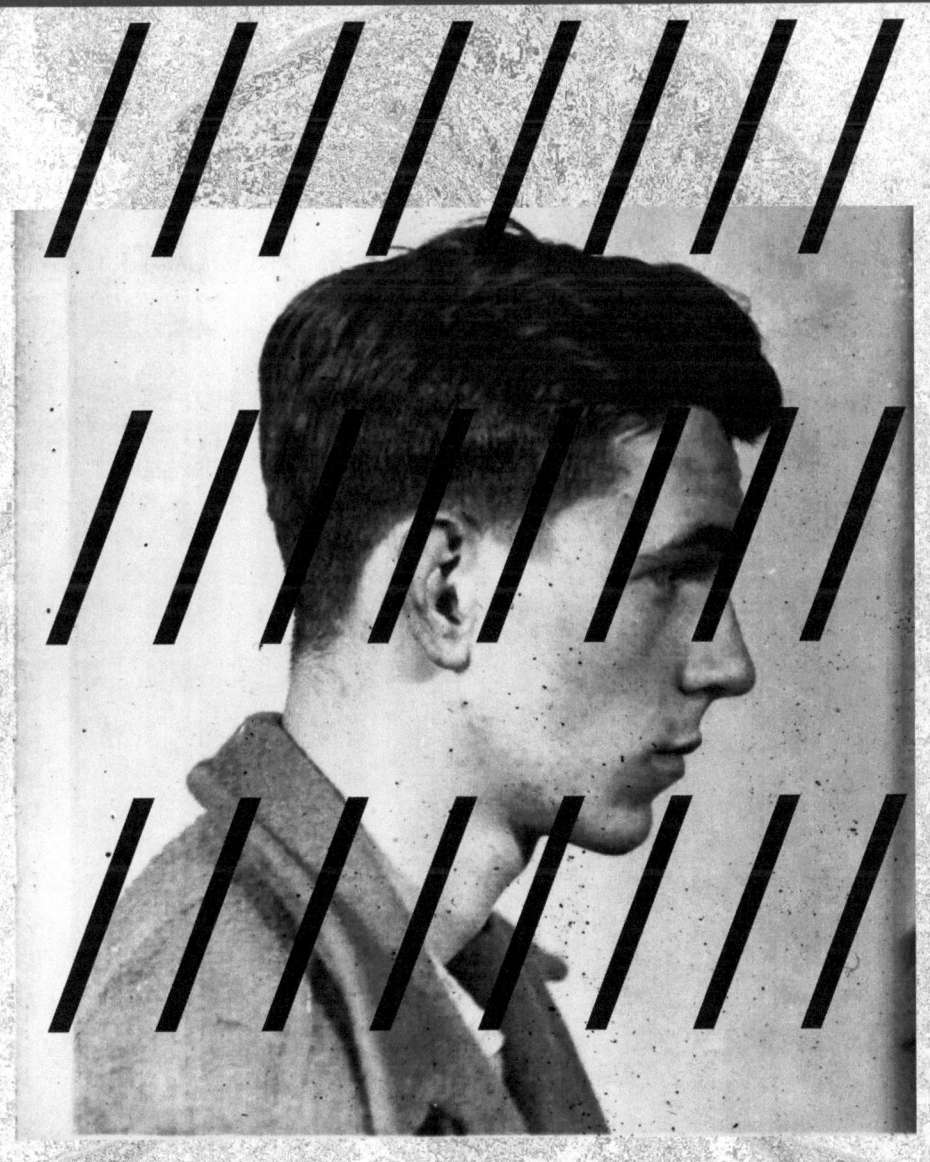

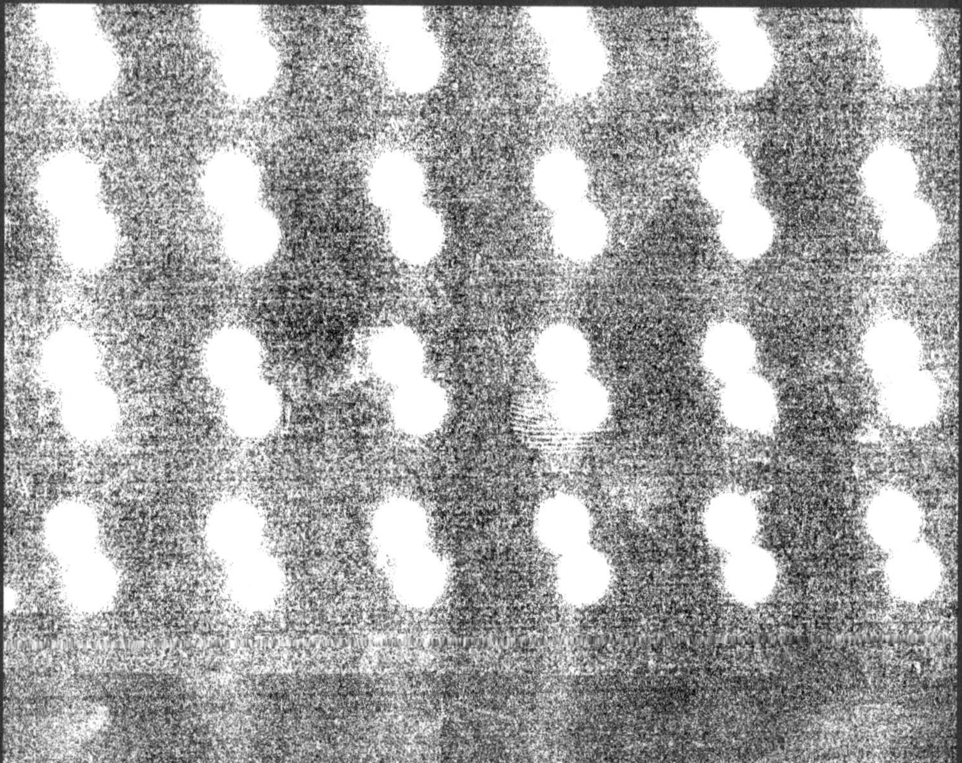

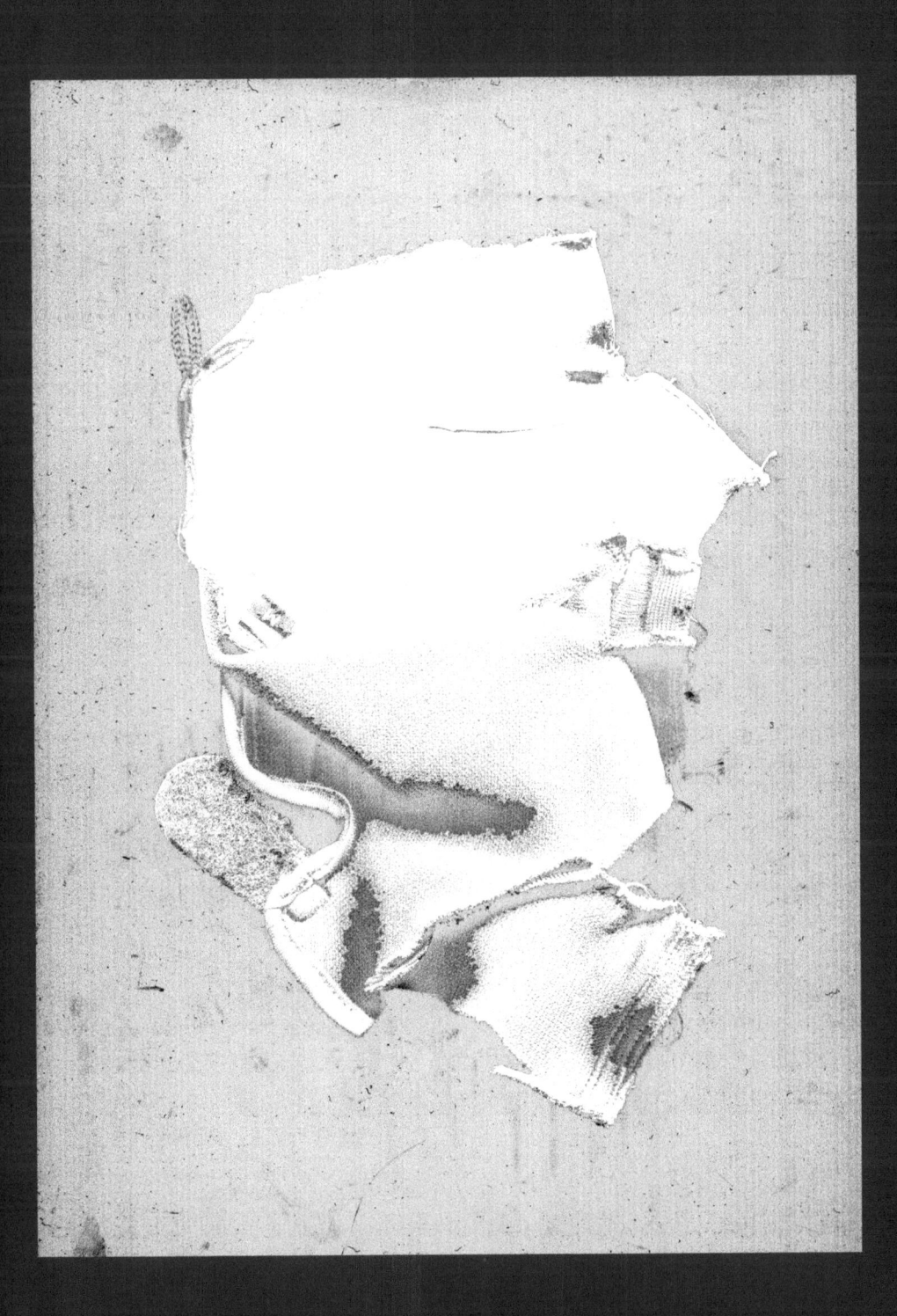

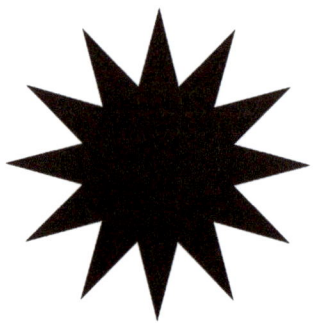
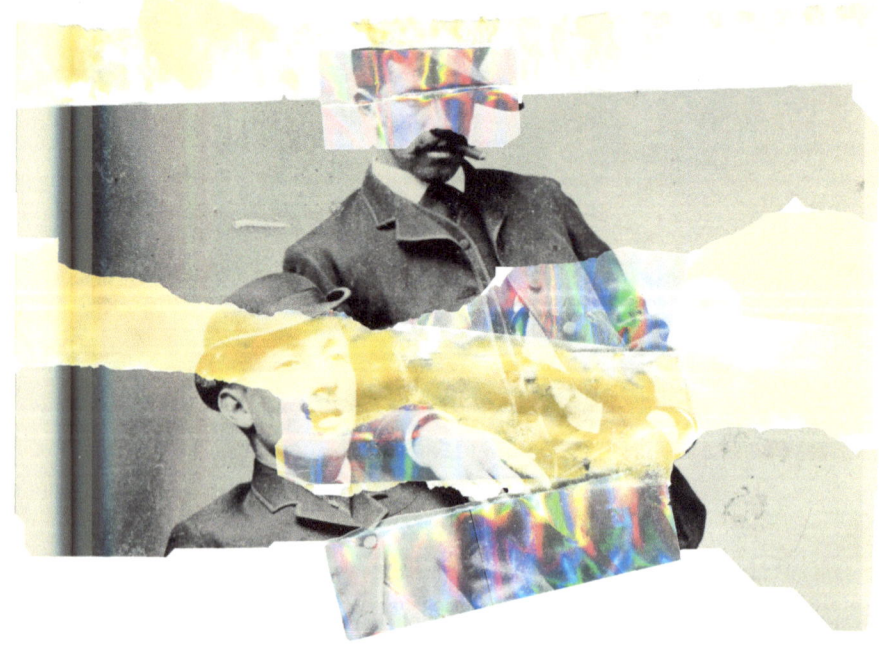

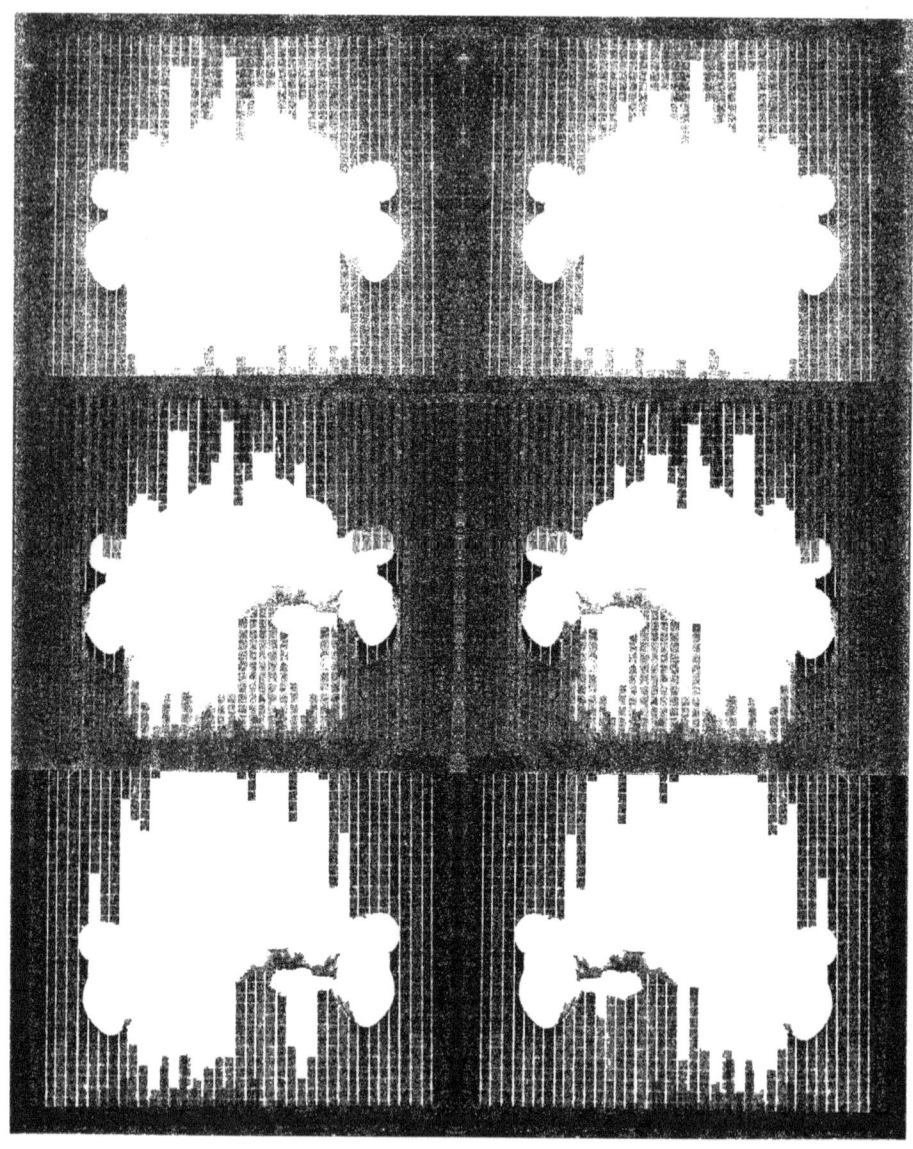

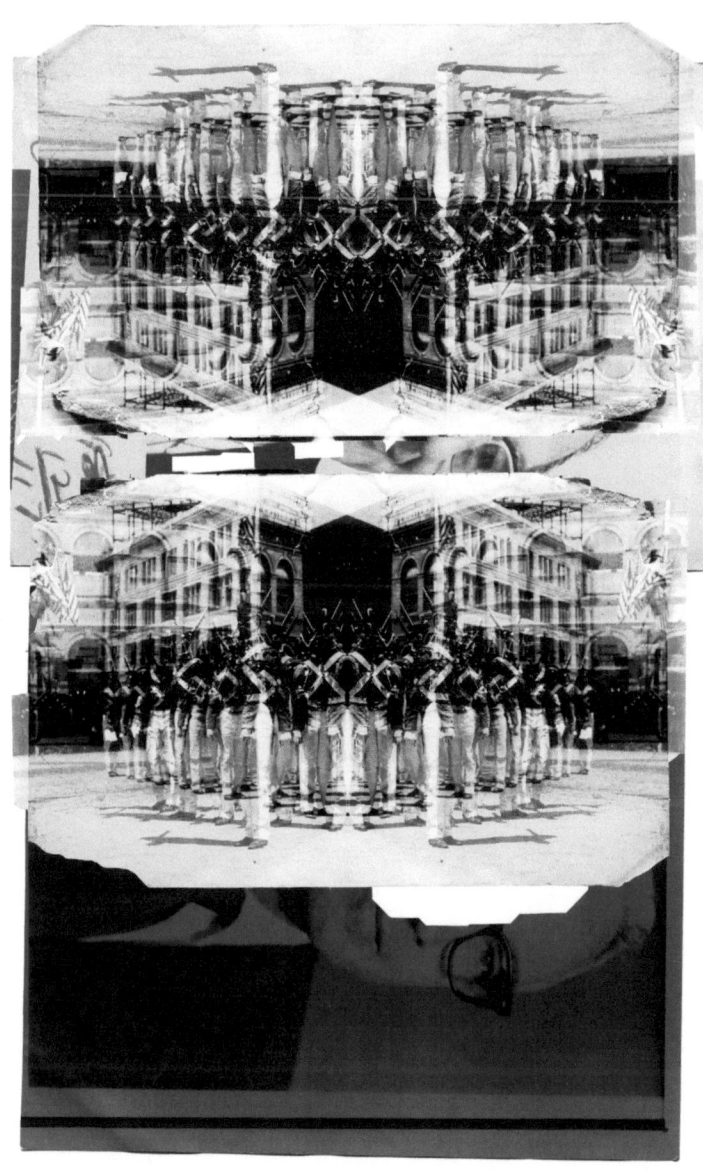

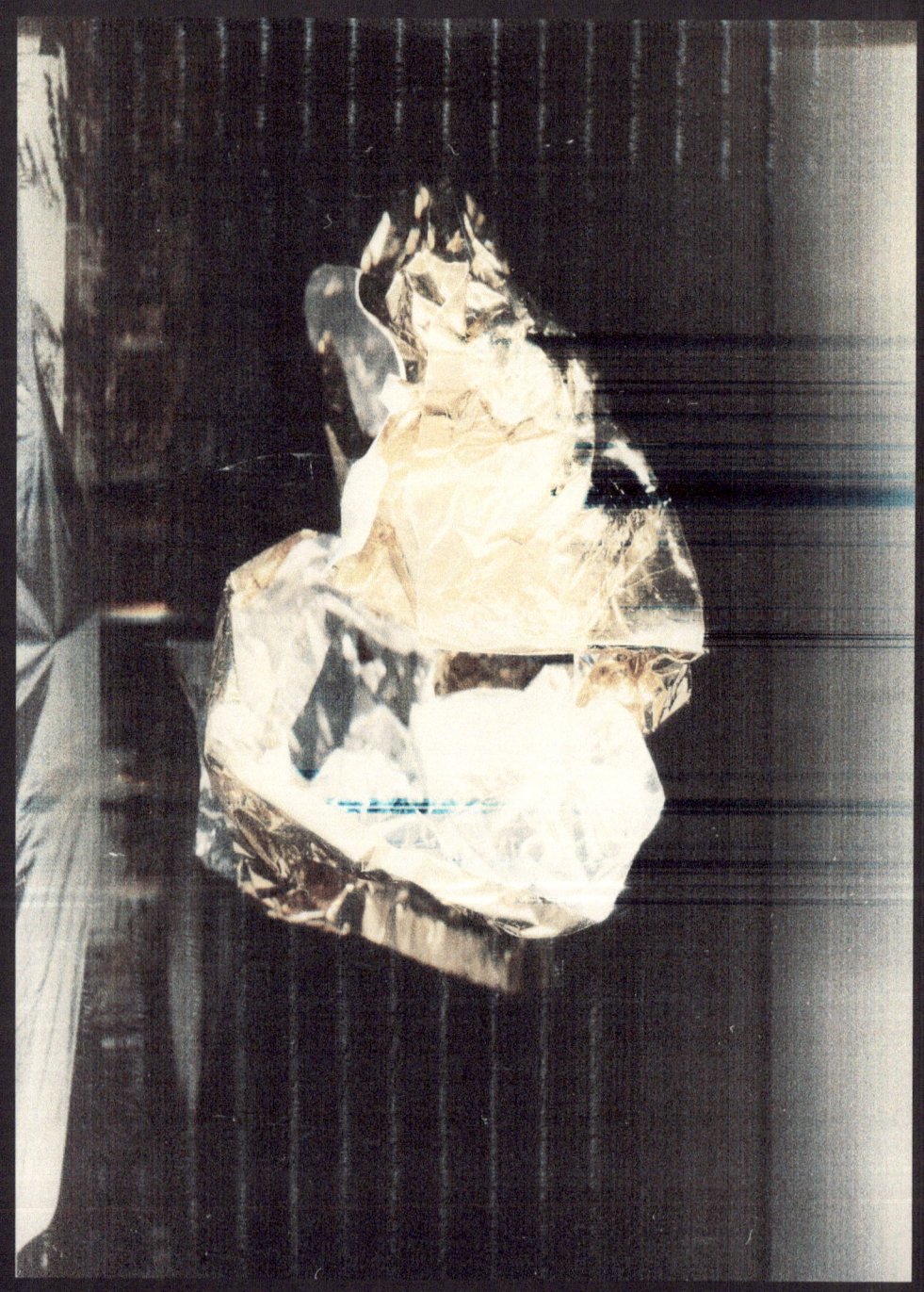

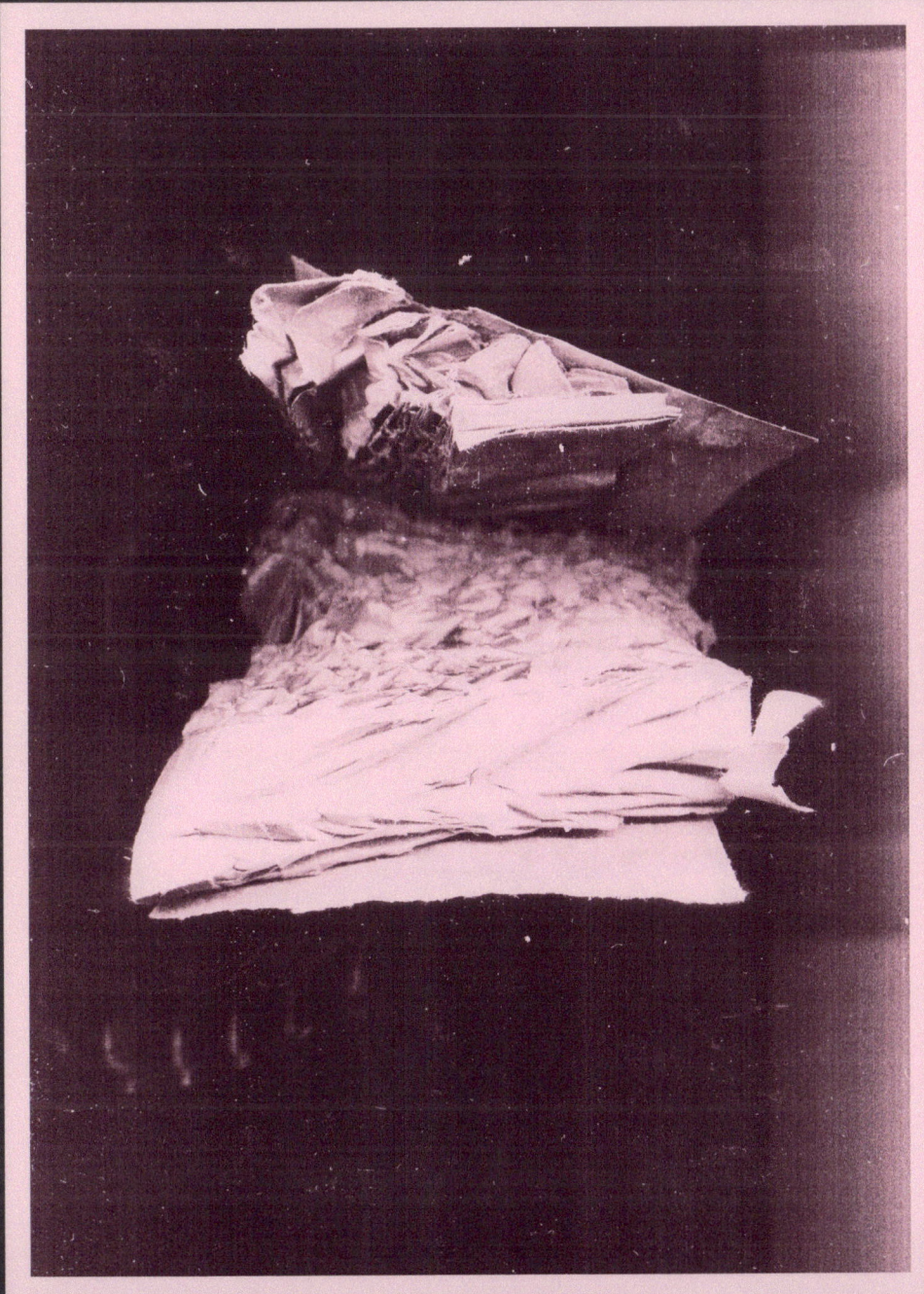

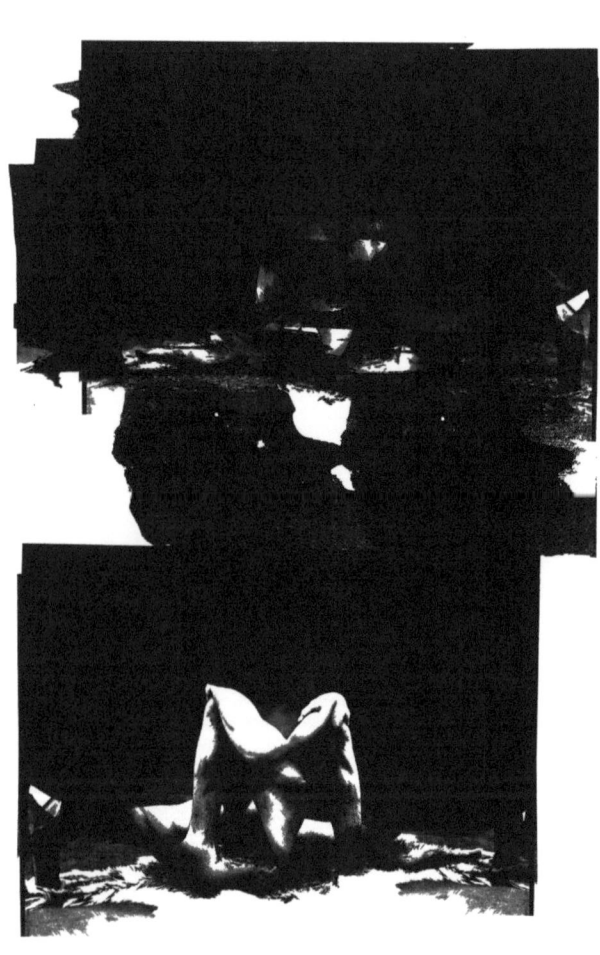

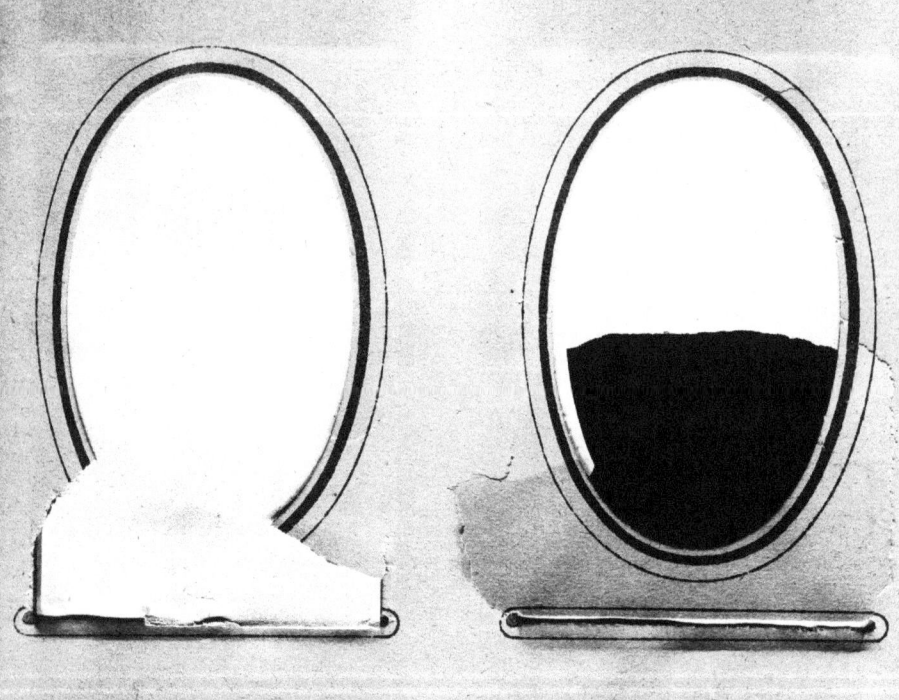

THE BEST DAD
I EVER HAD

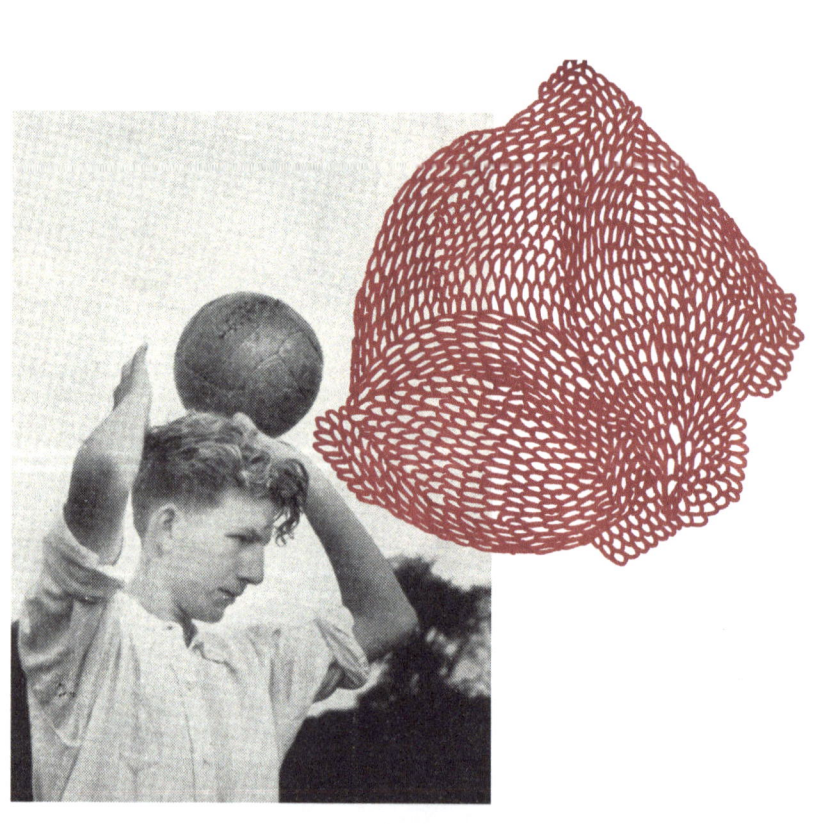

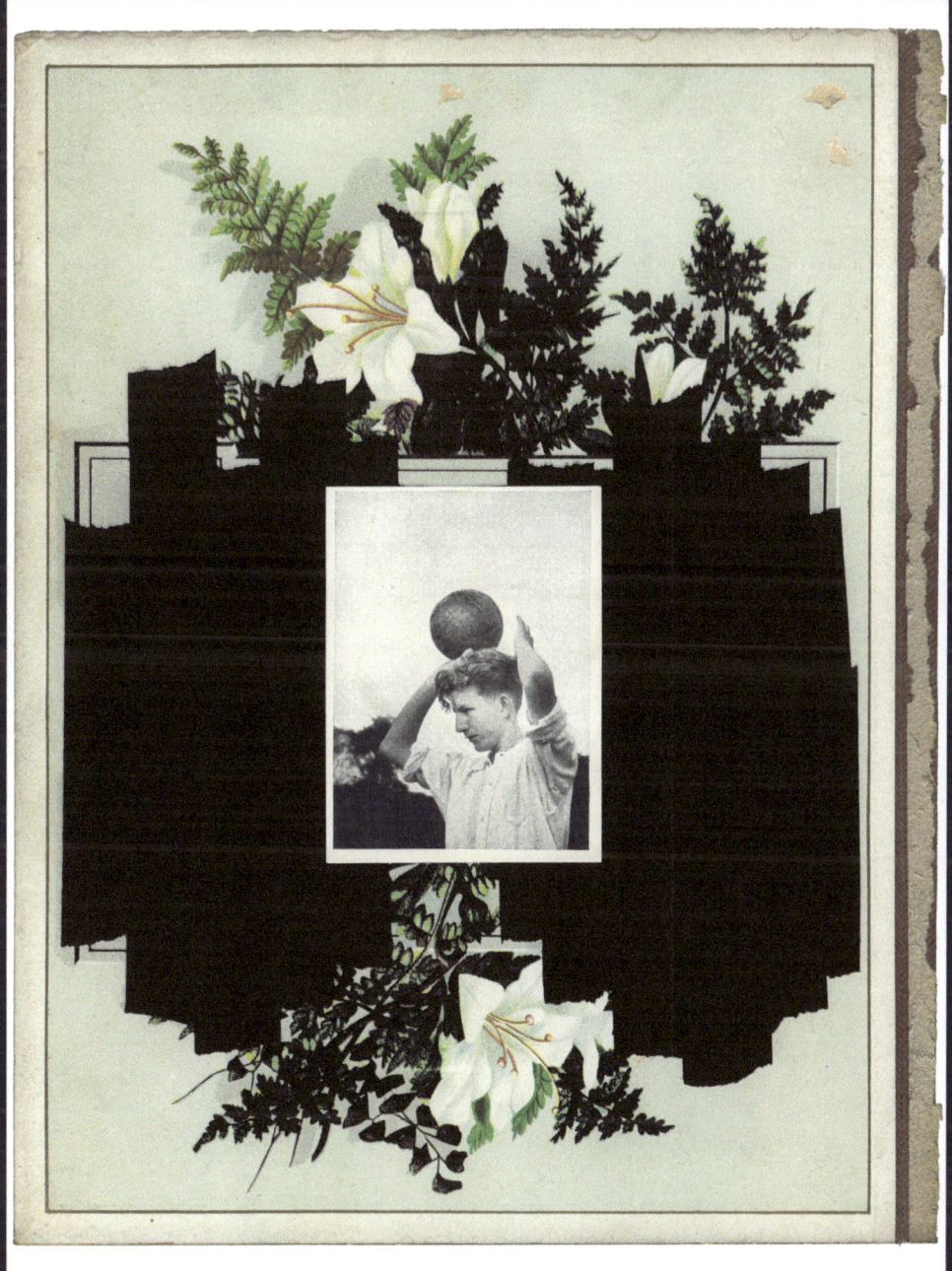

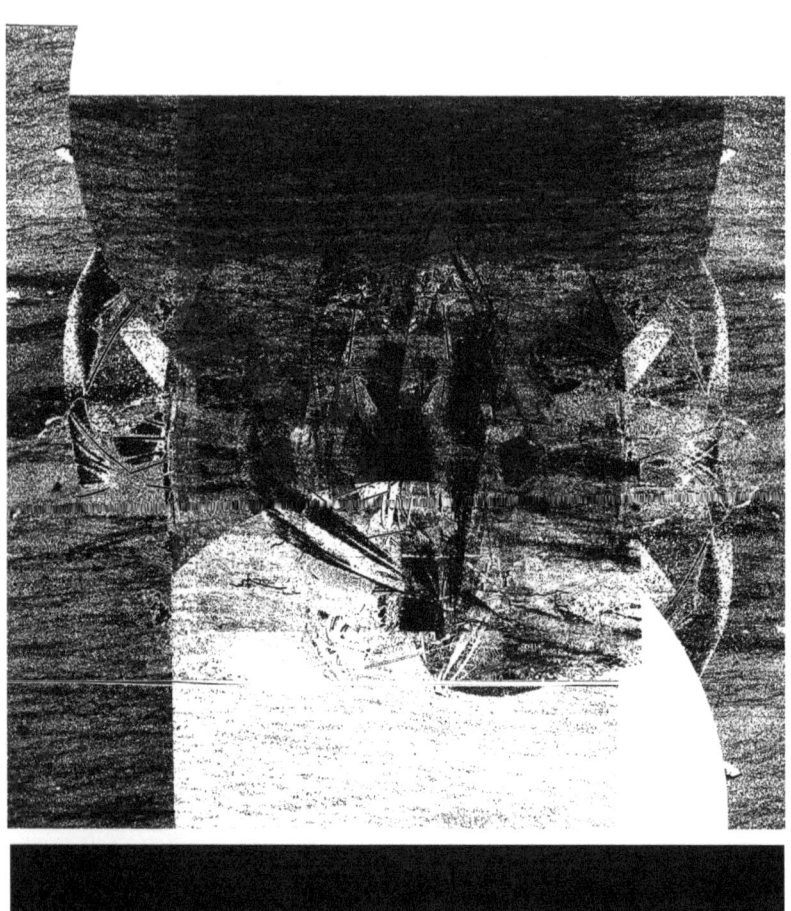

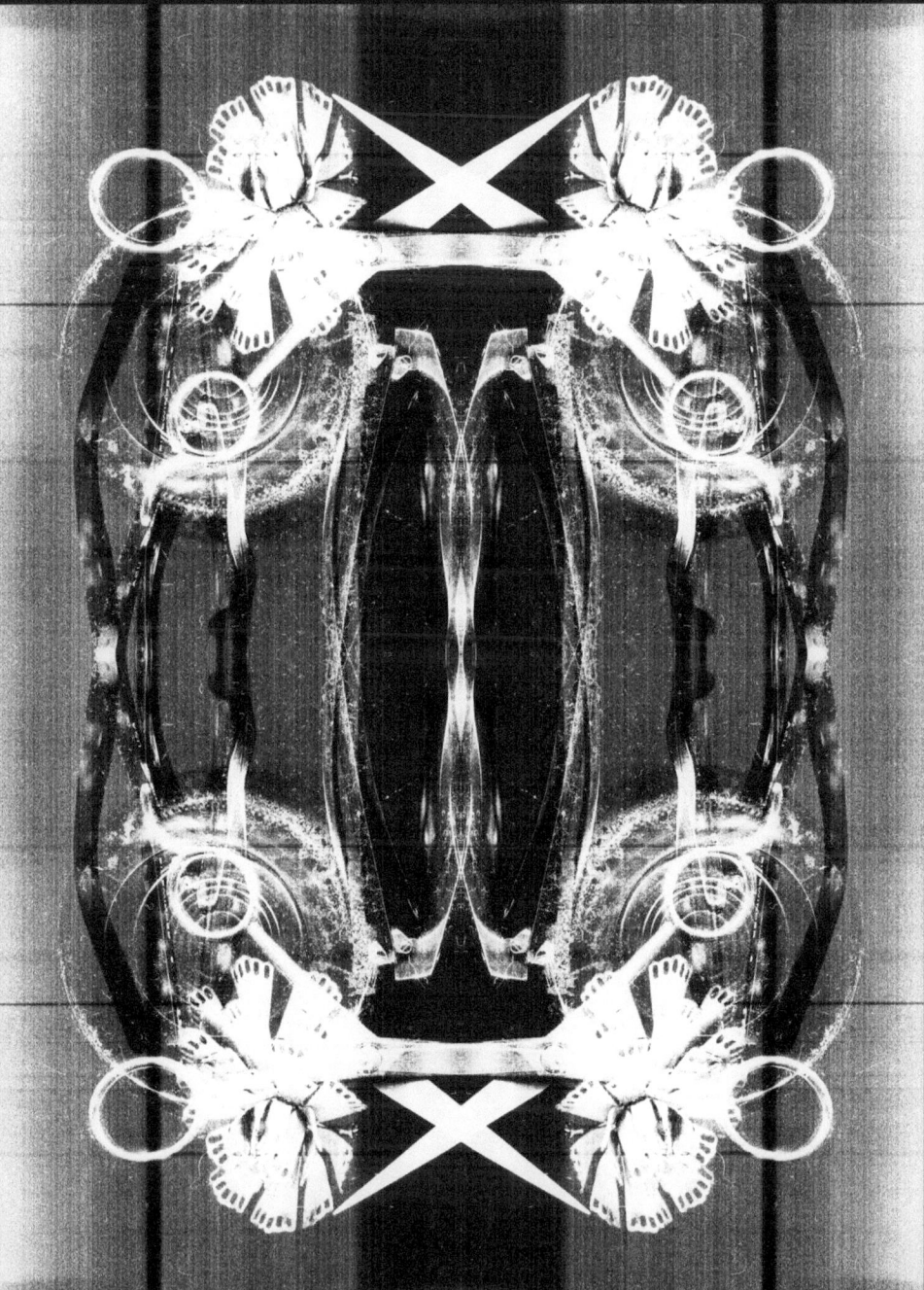

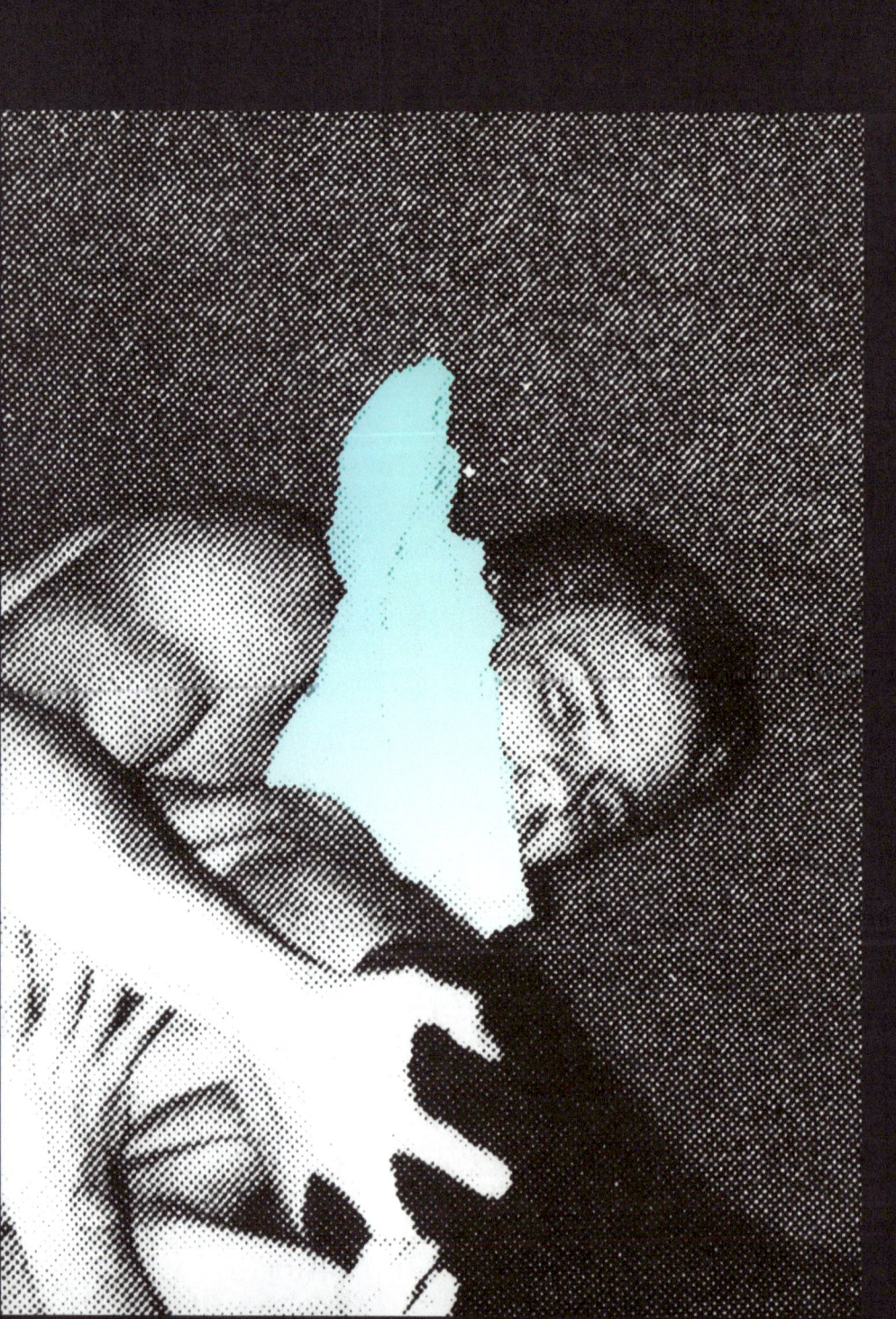

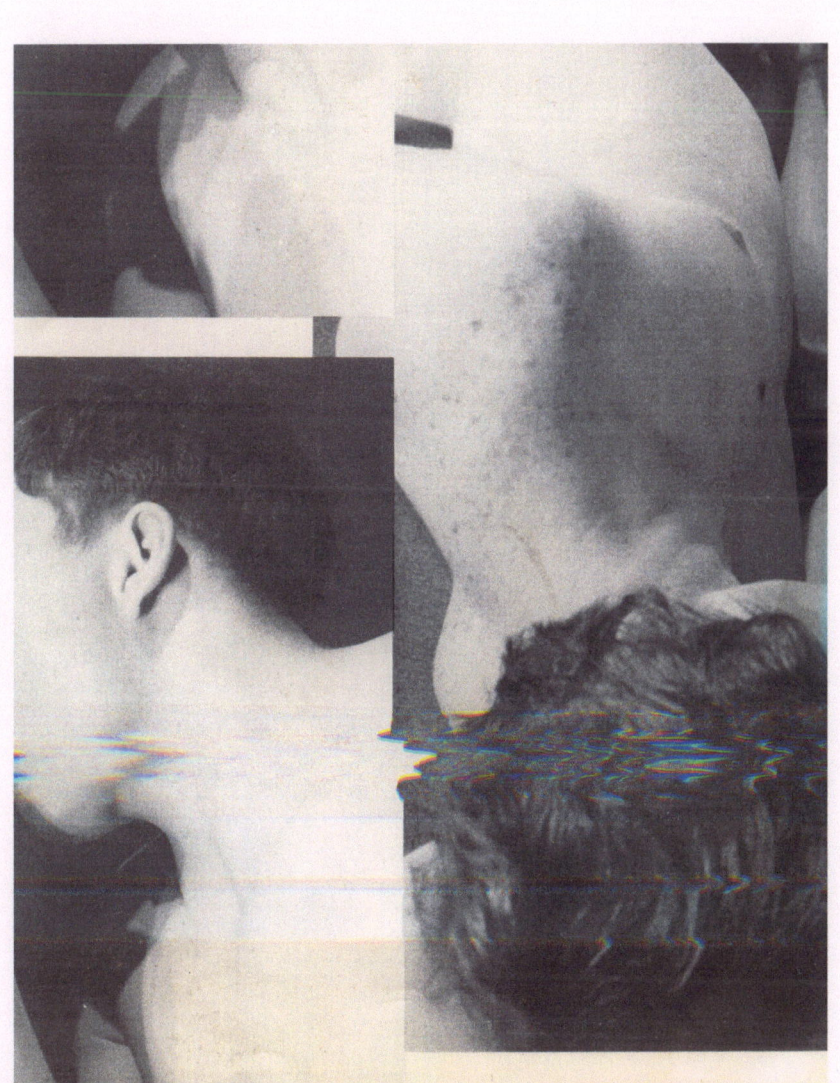

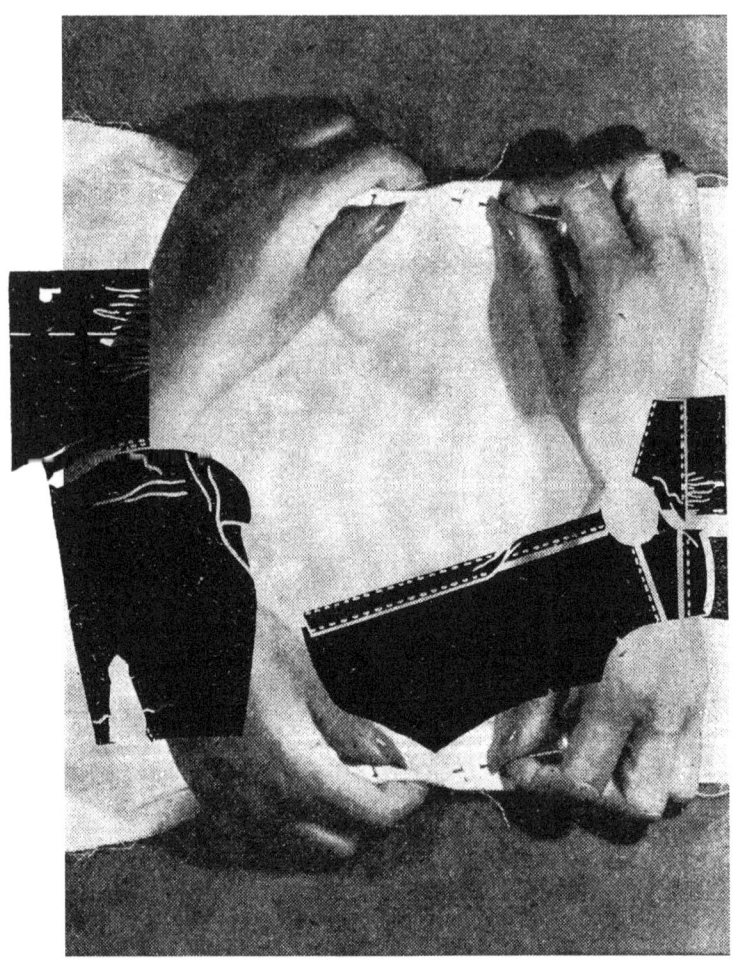

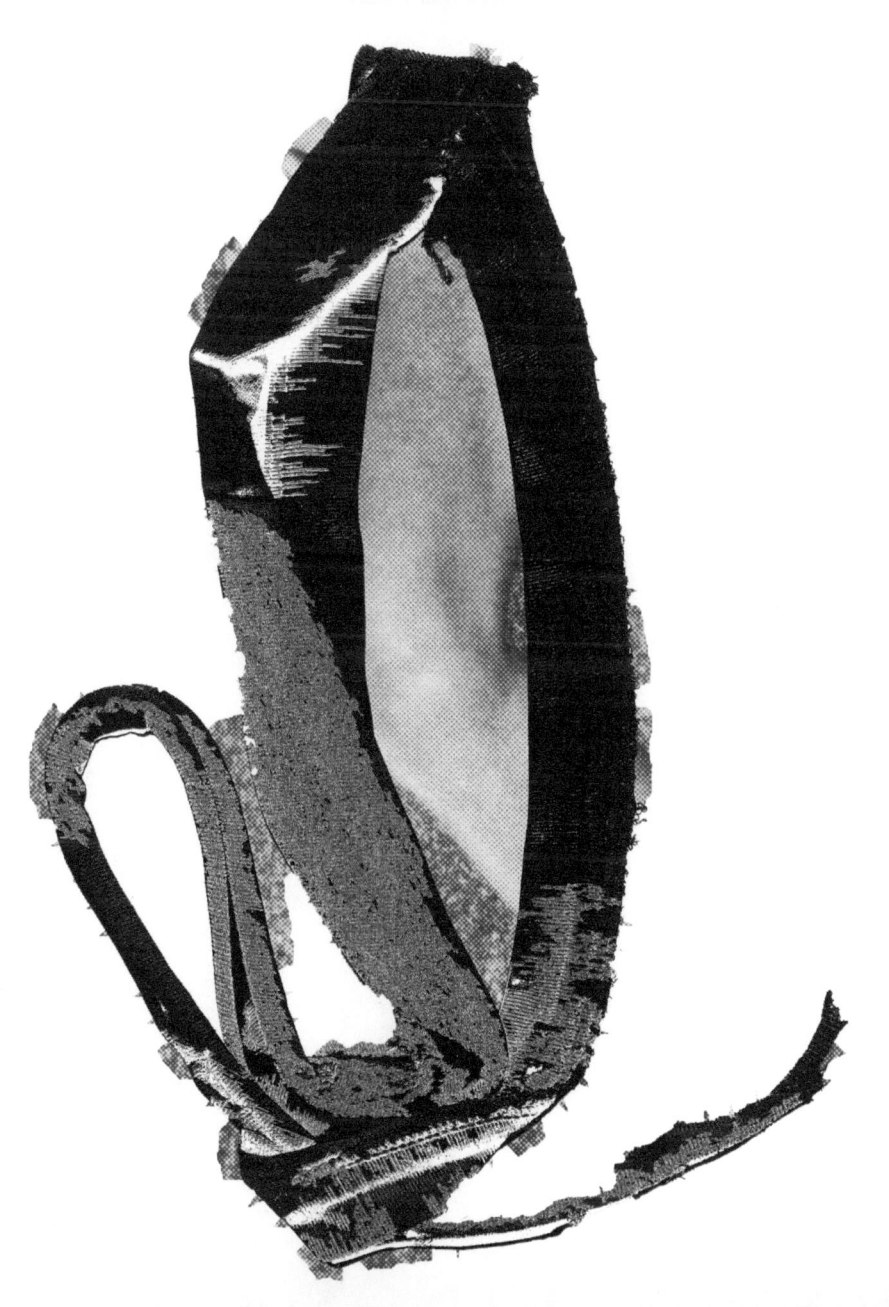

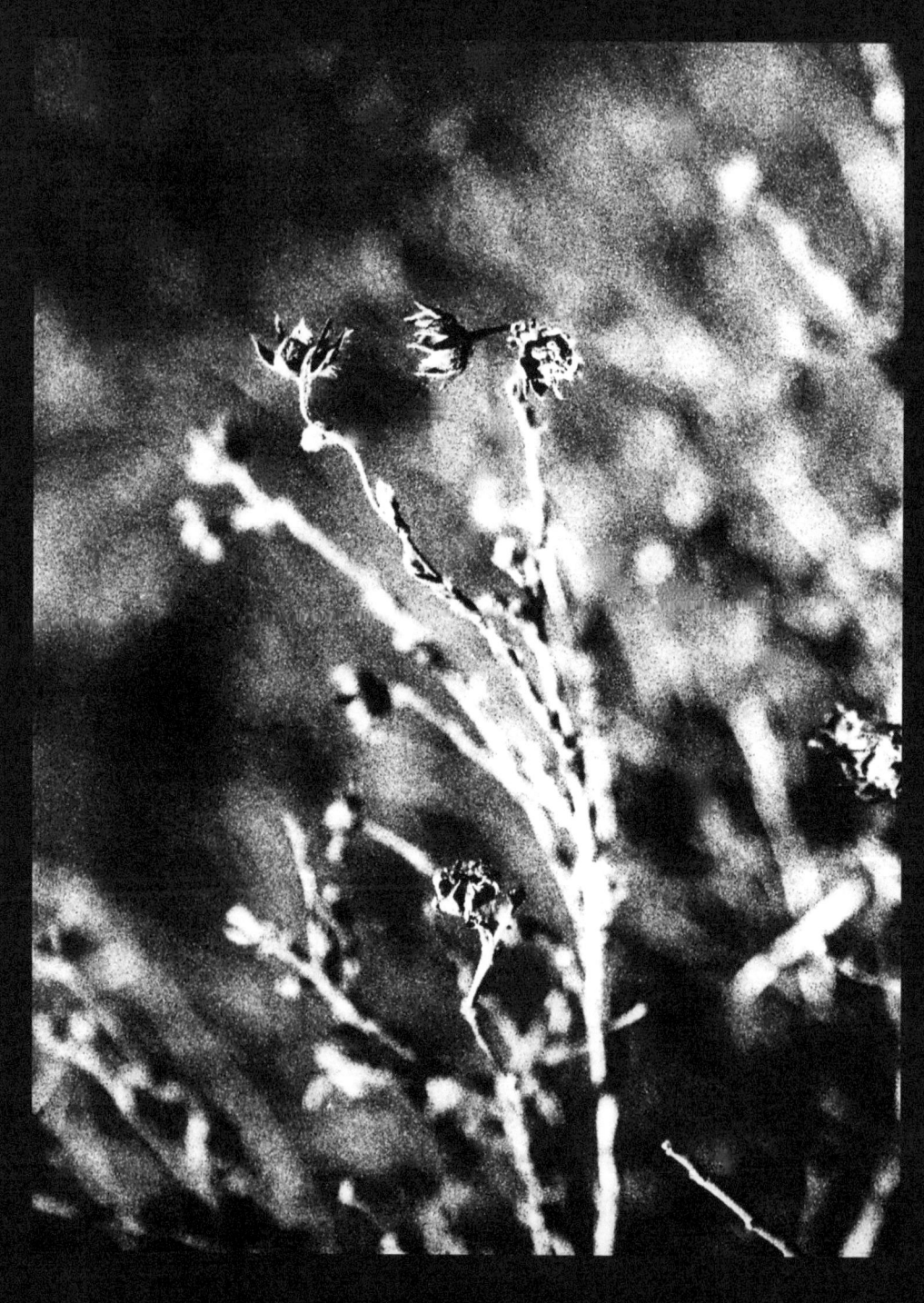

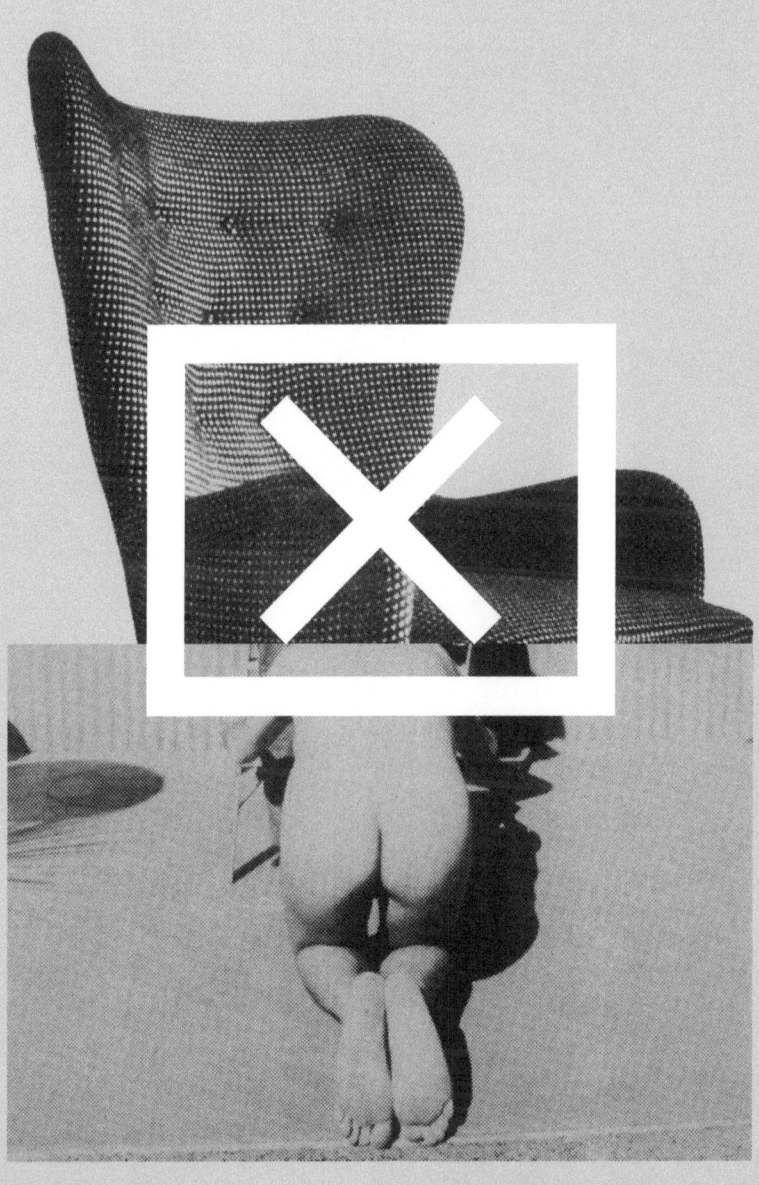

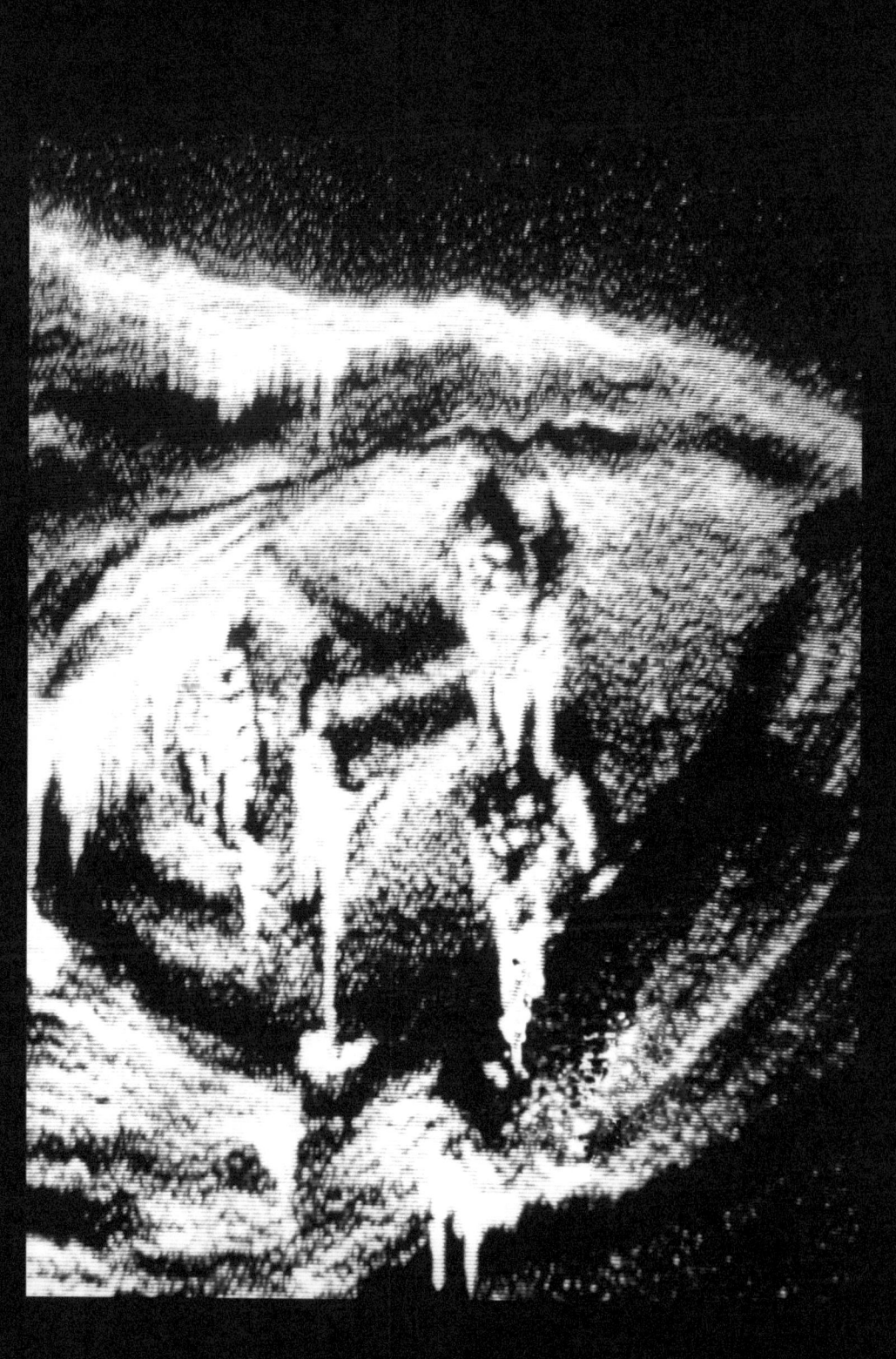

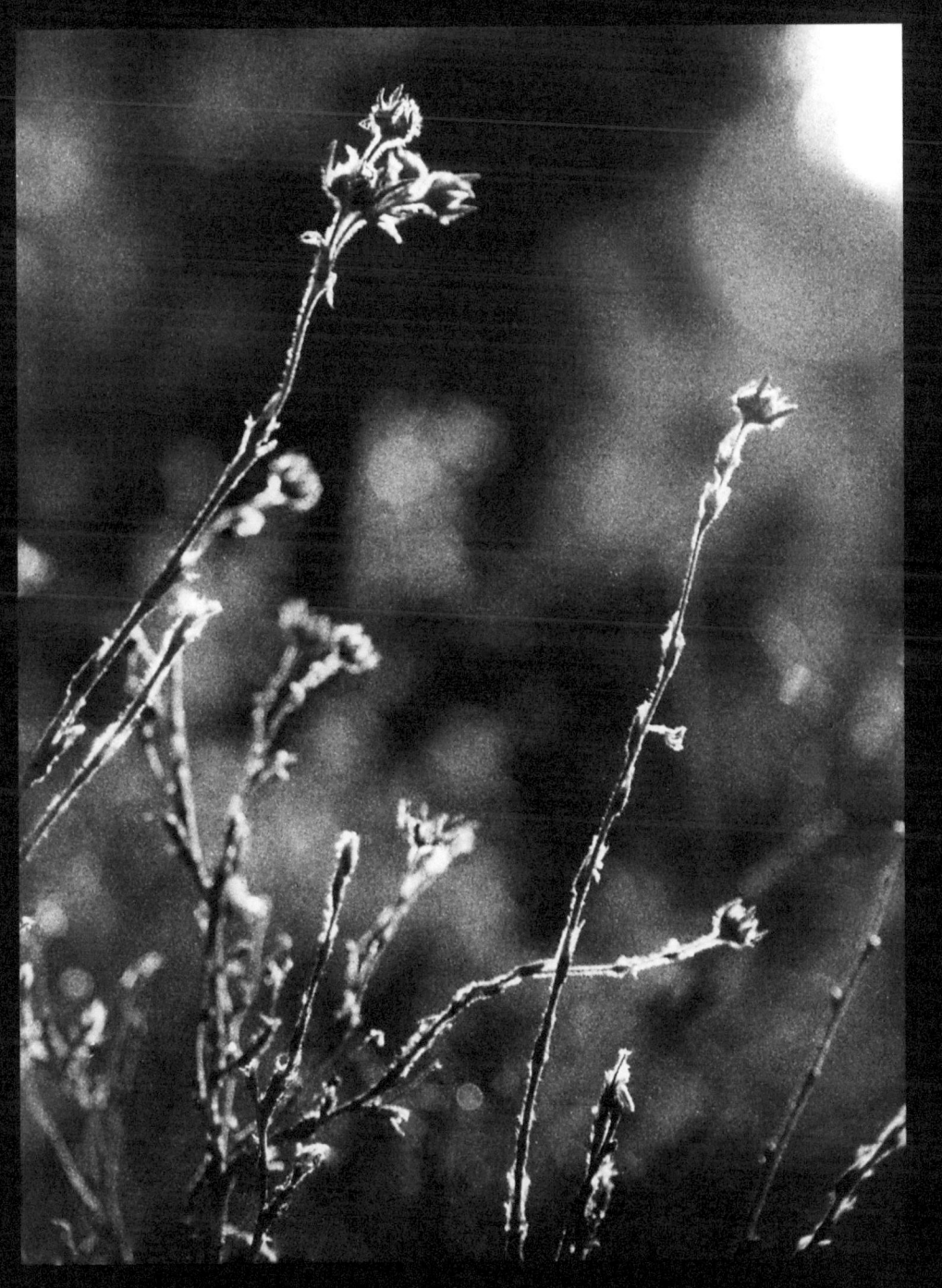

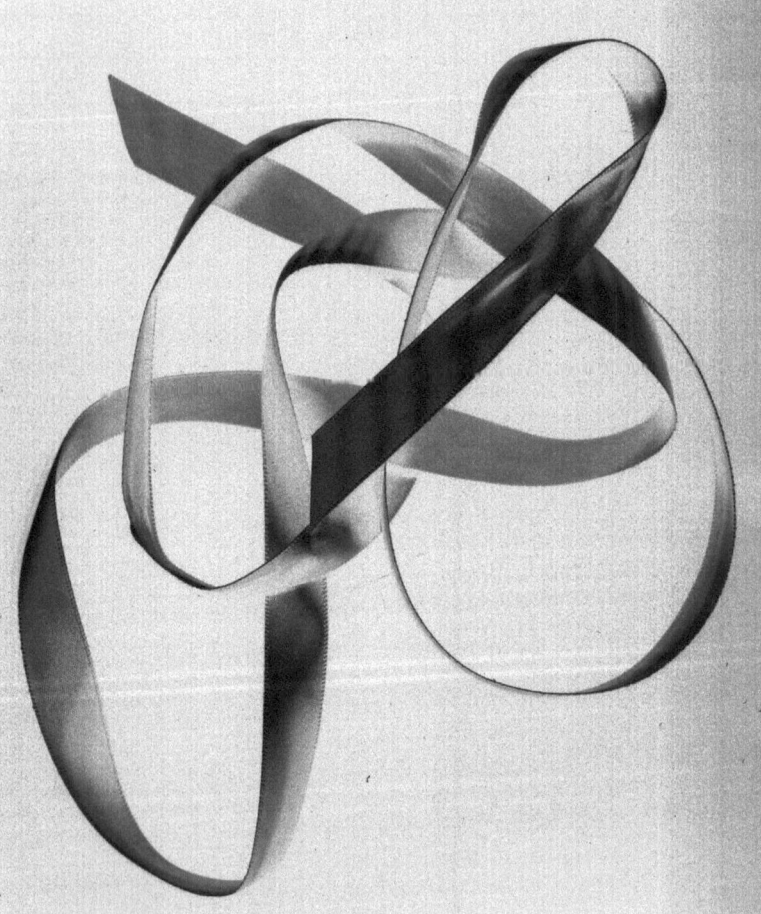

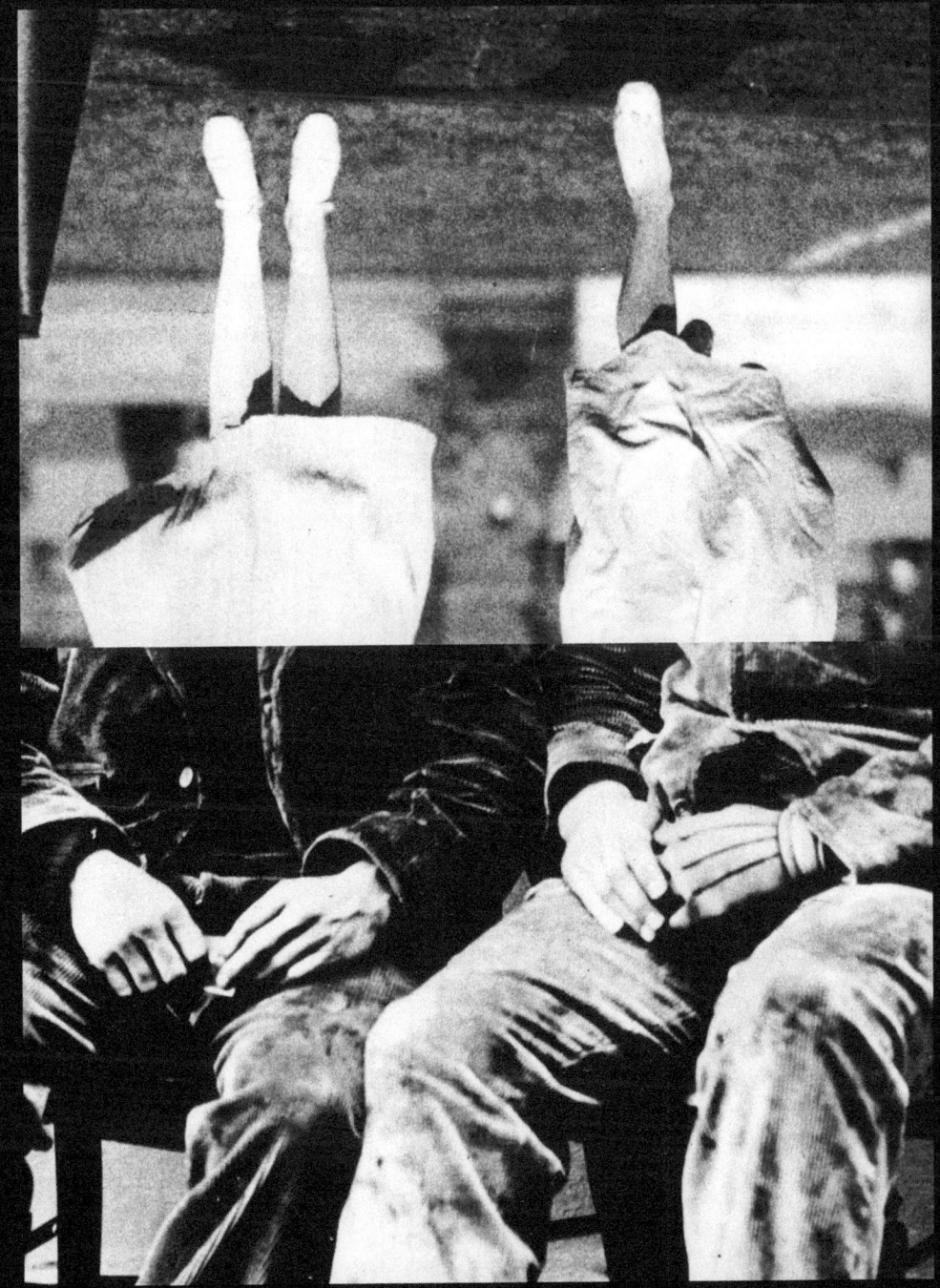

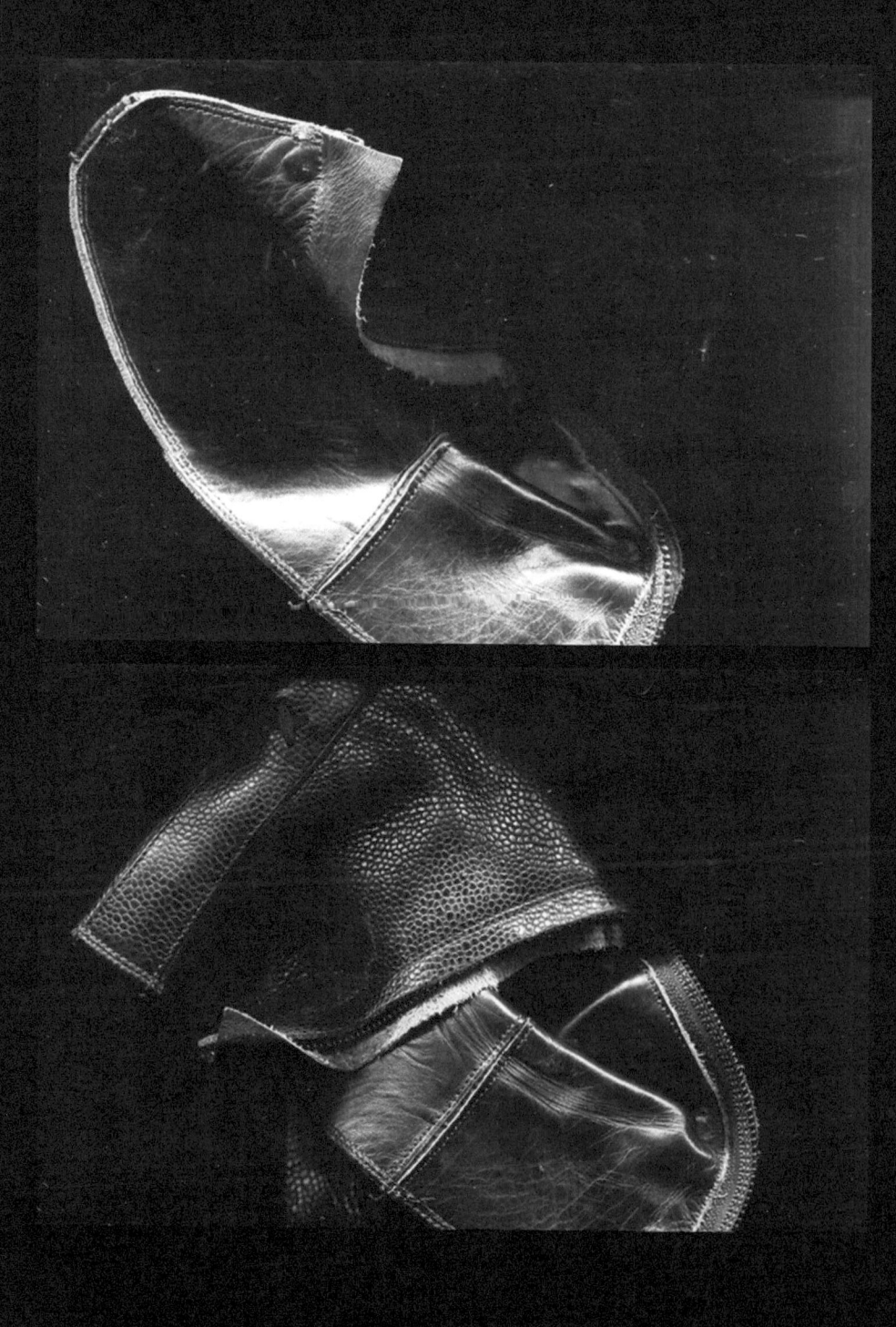

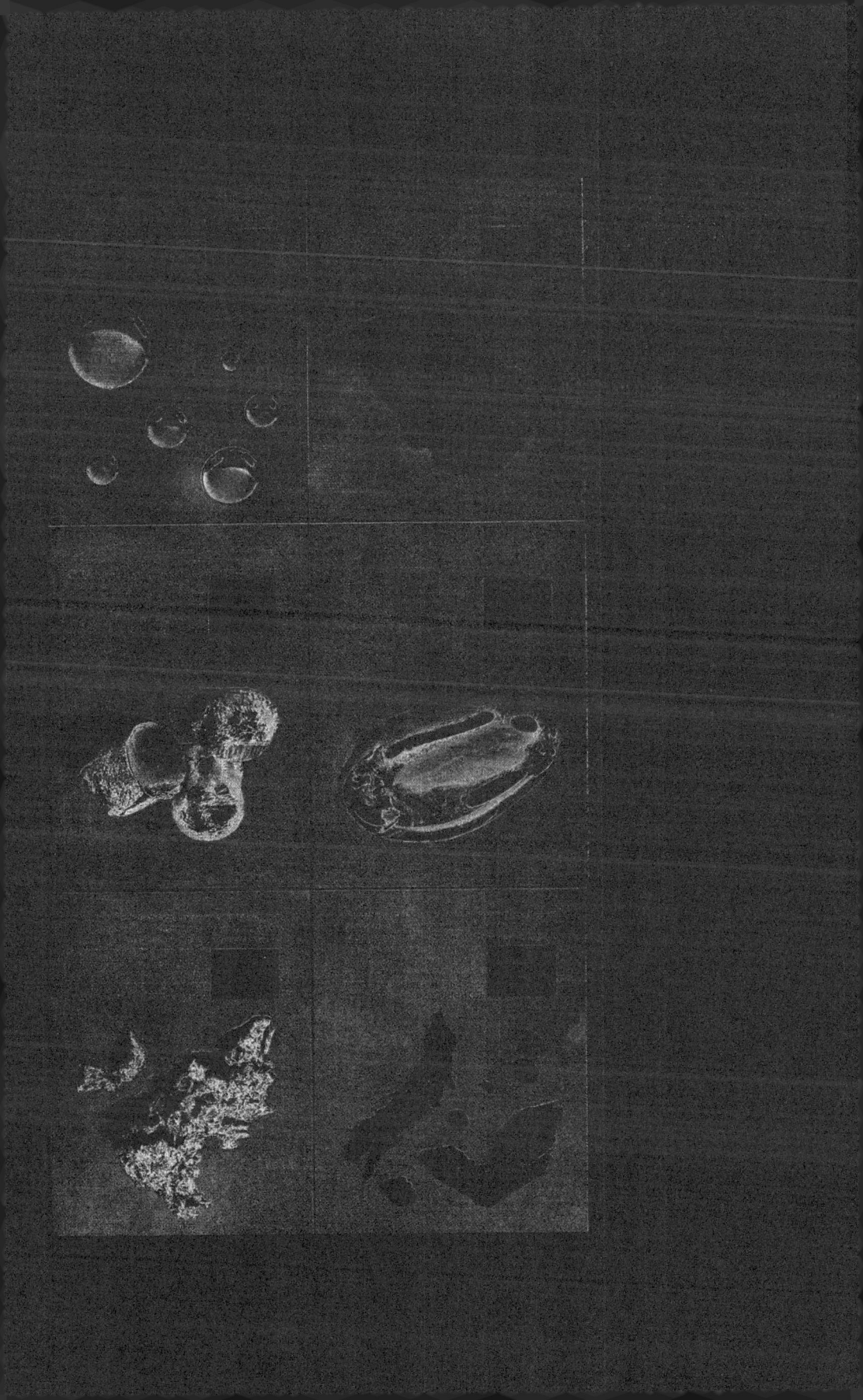

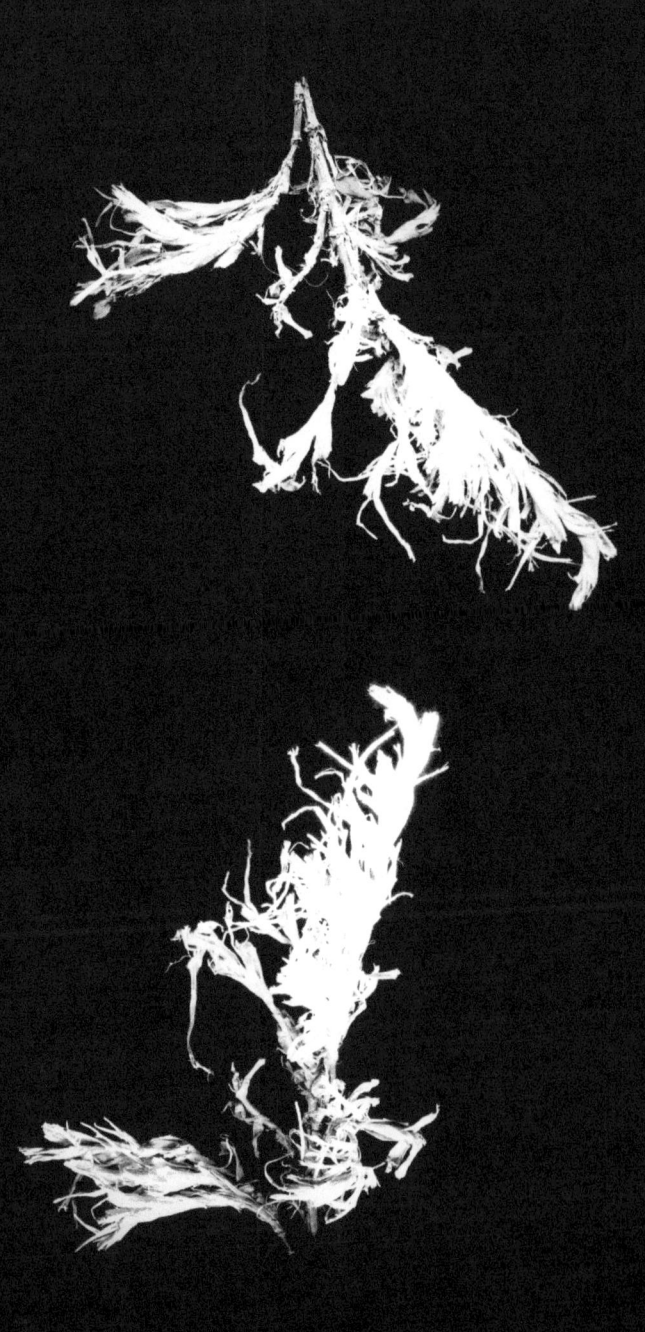

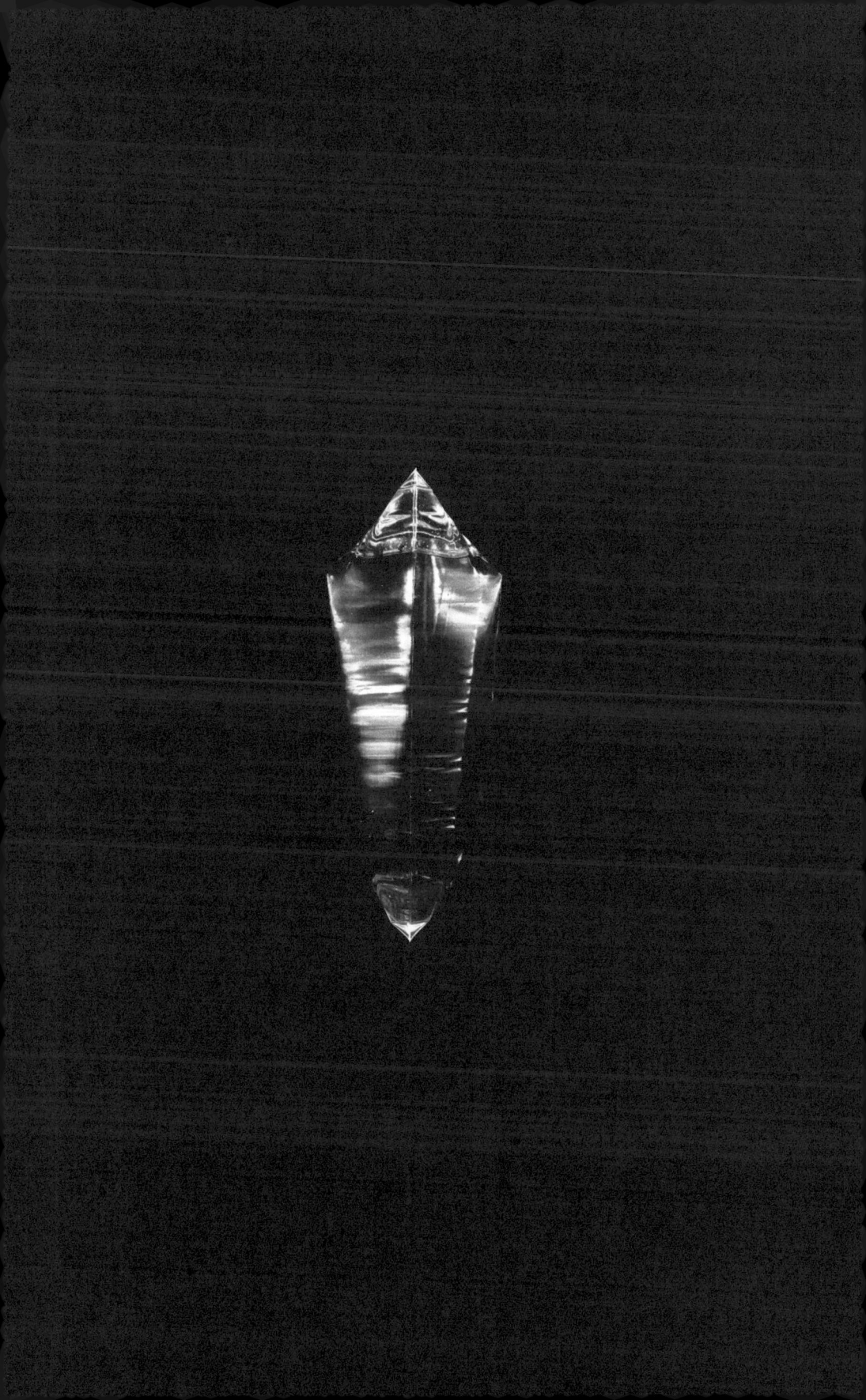

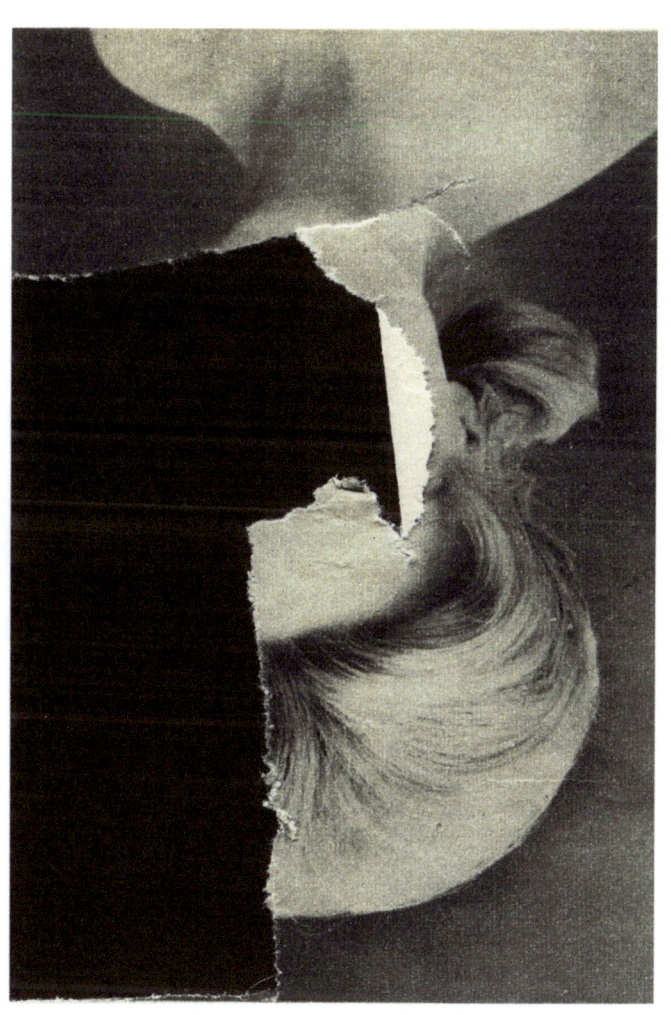

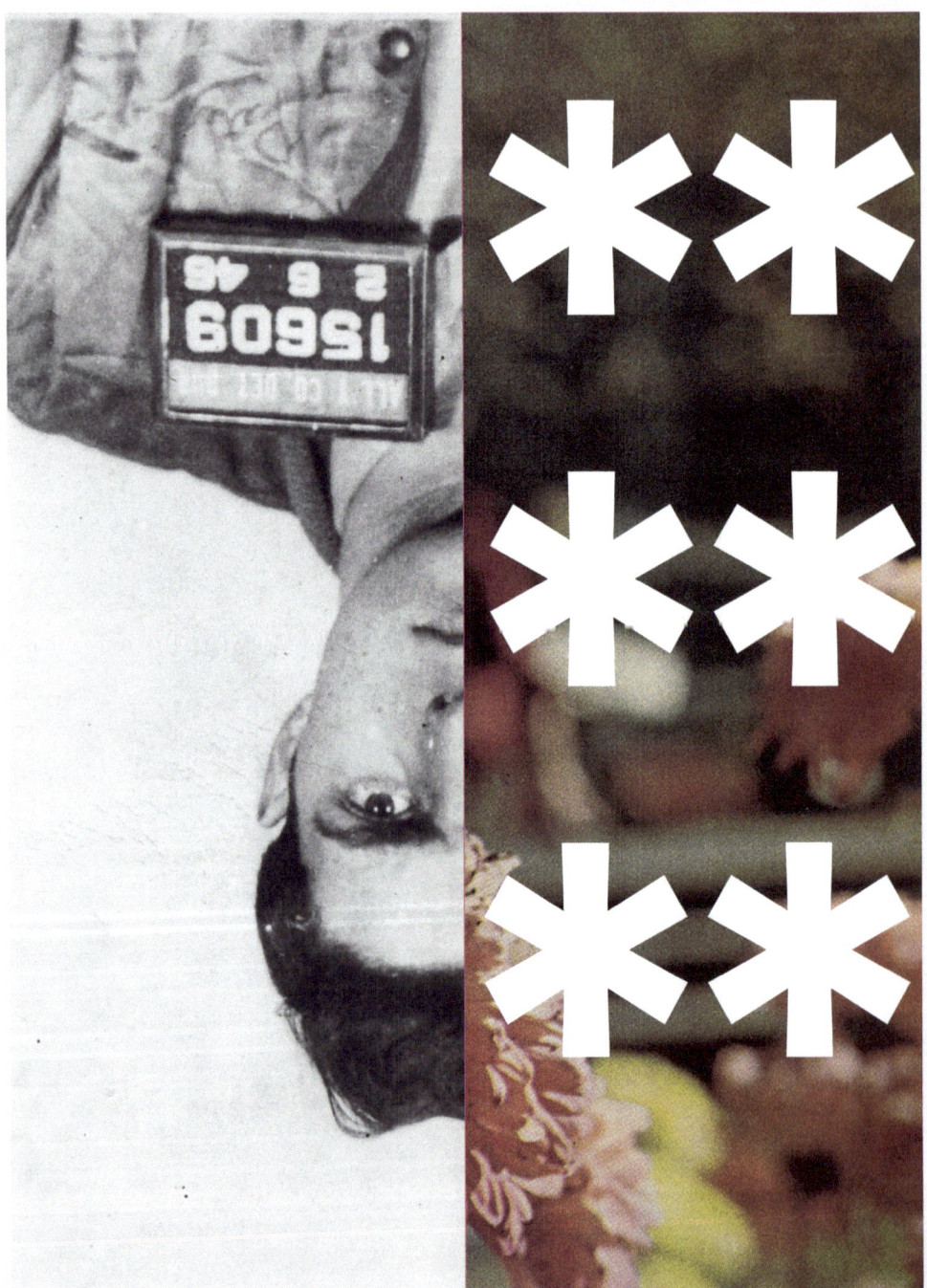

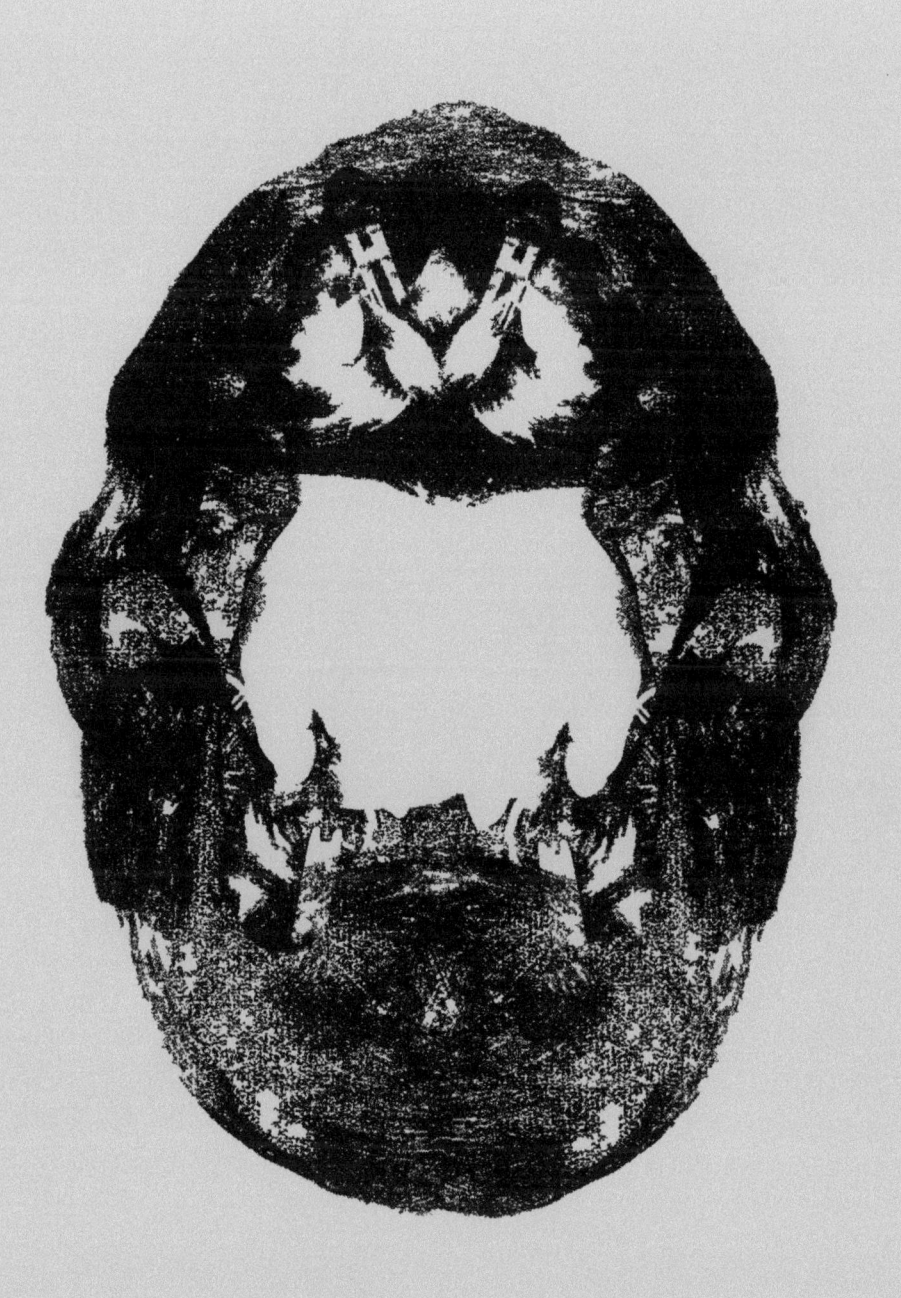

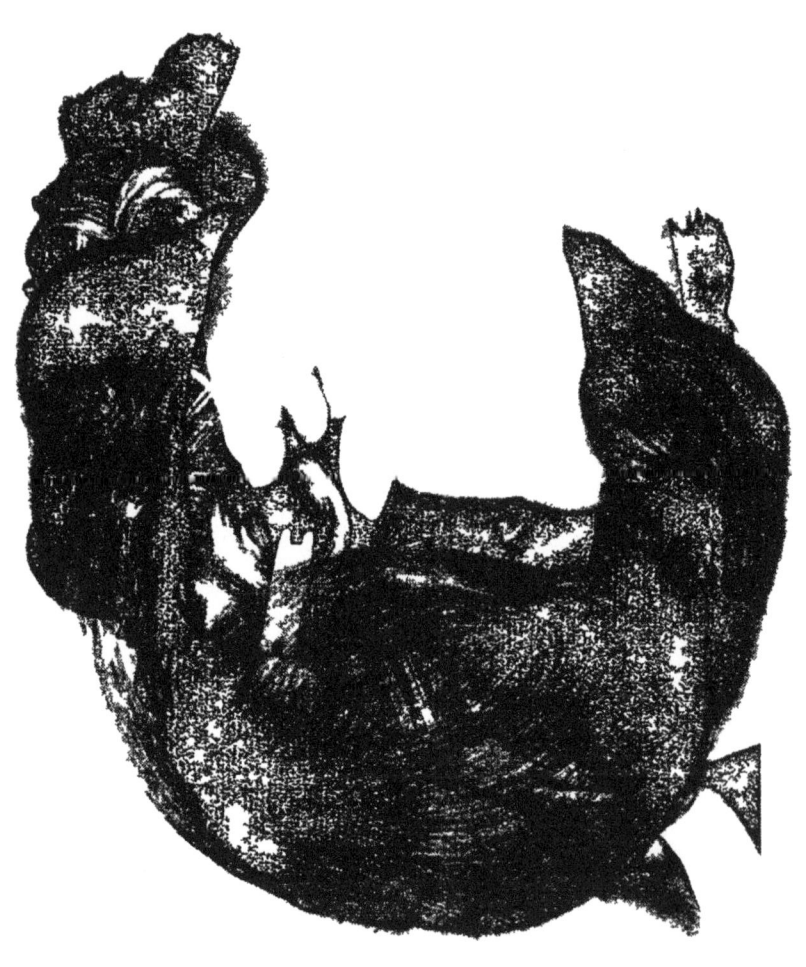

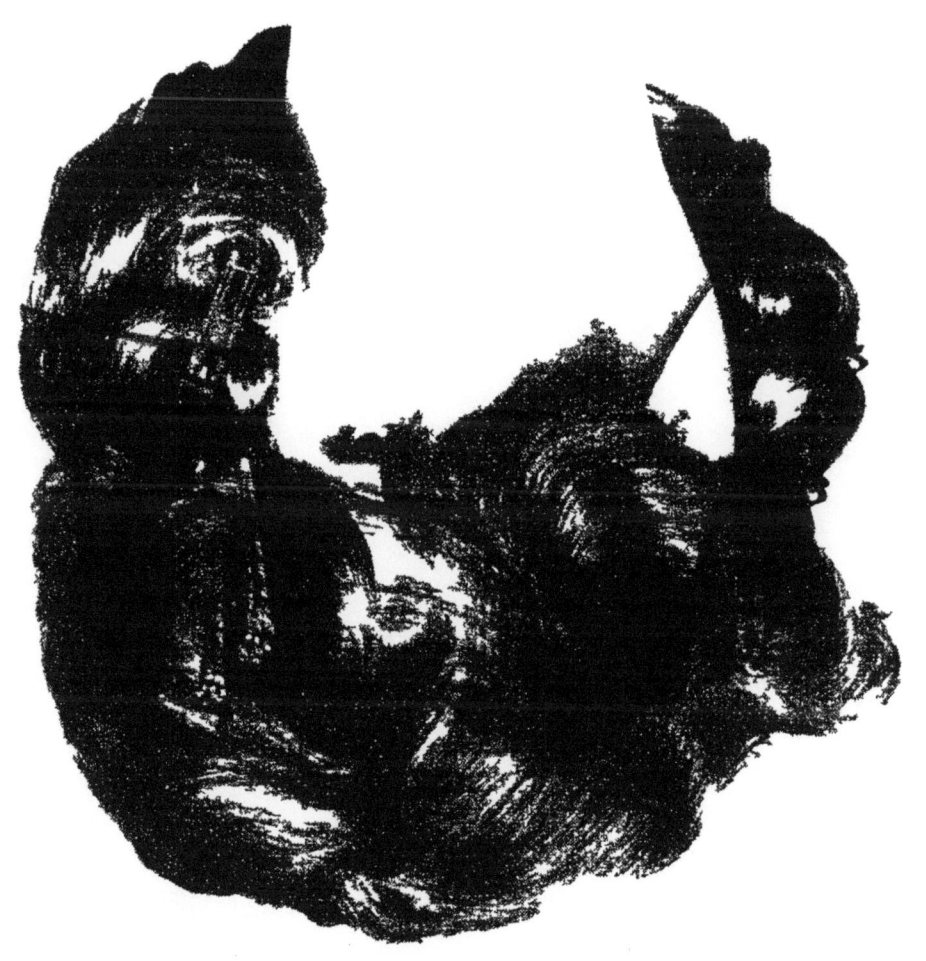

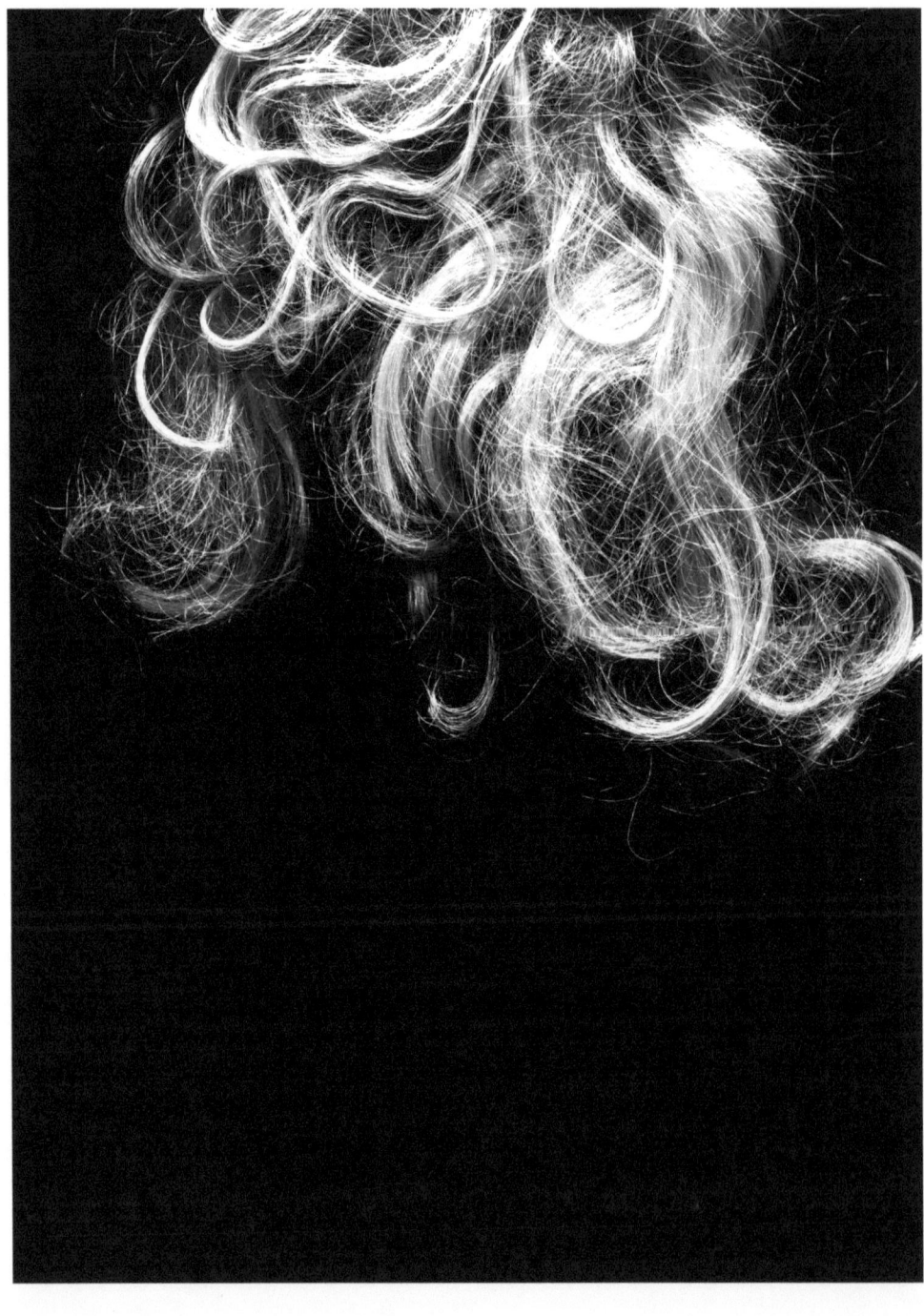

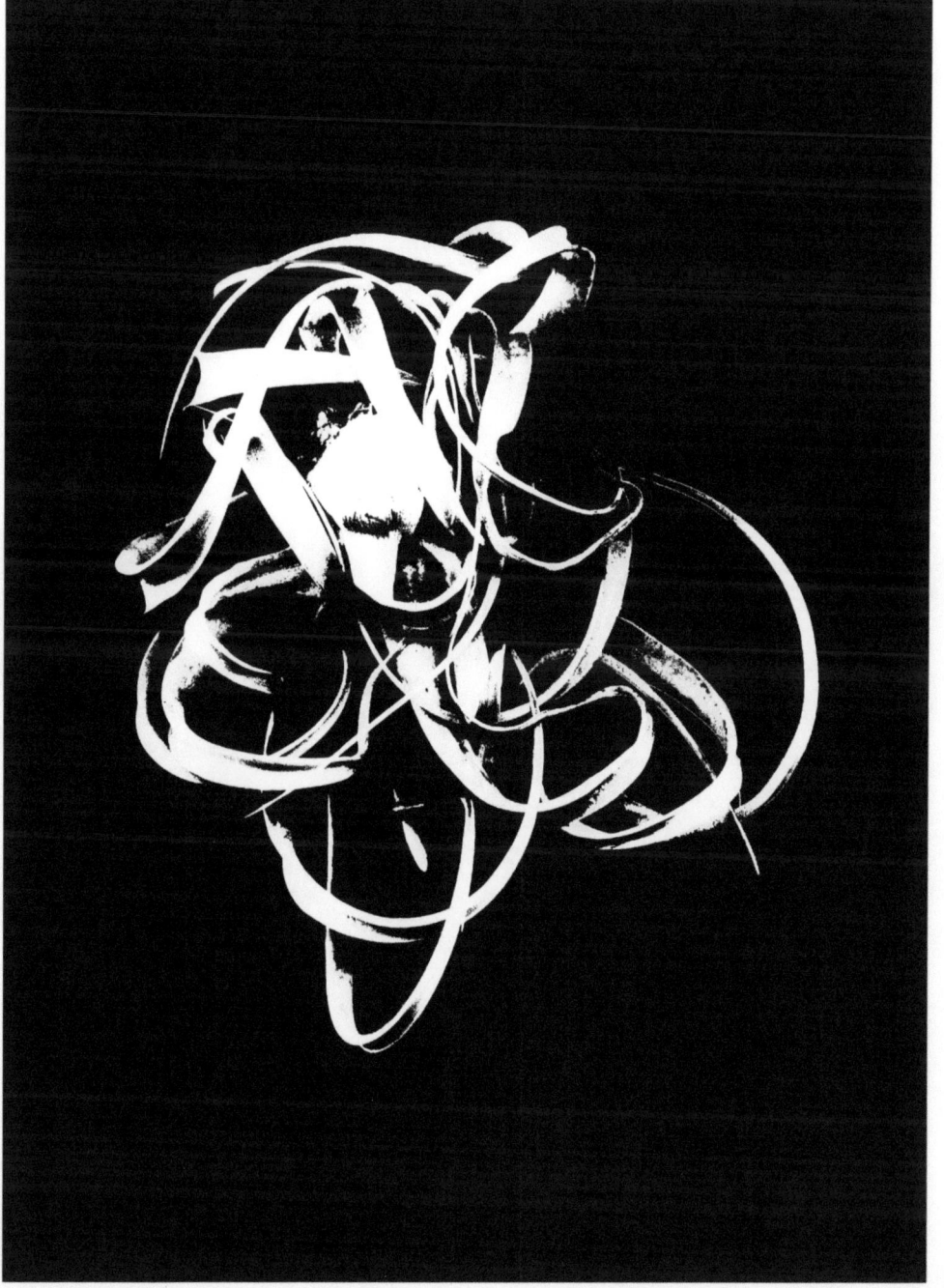

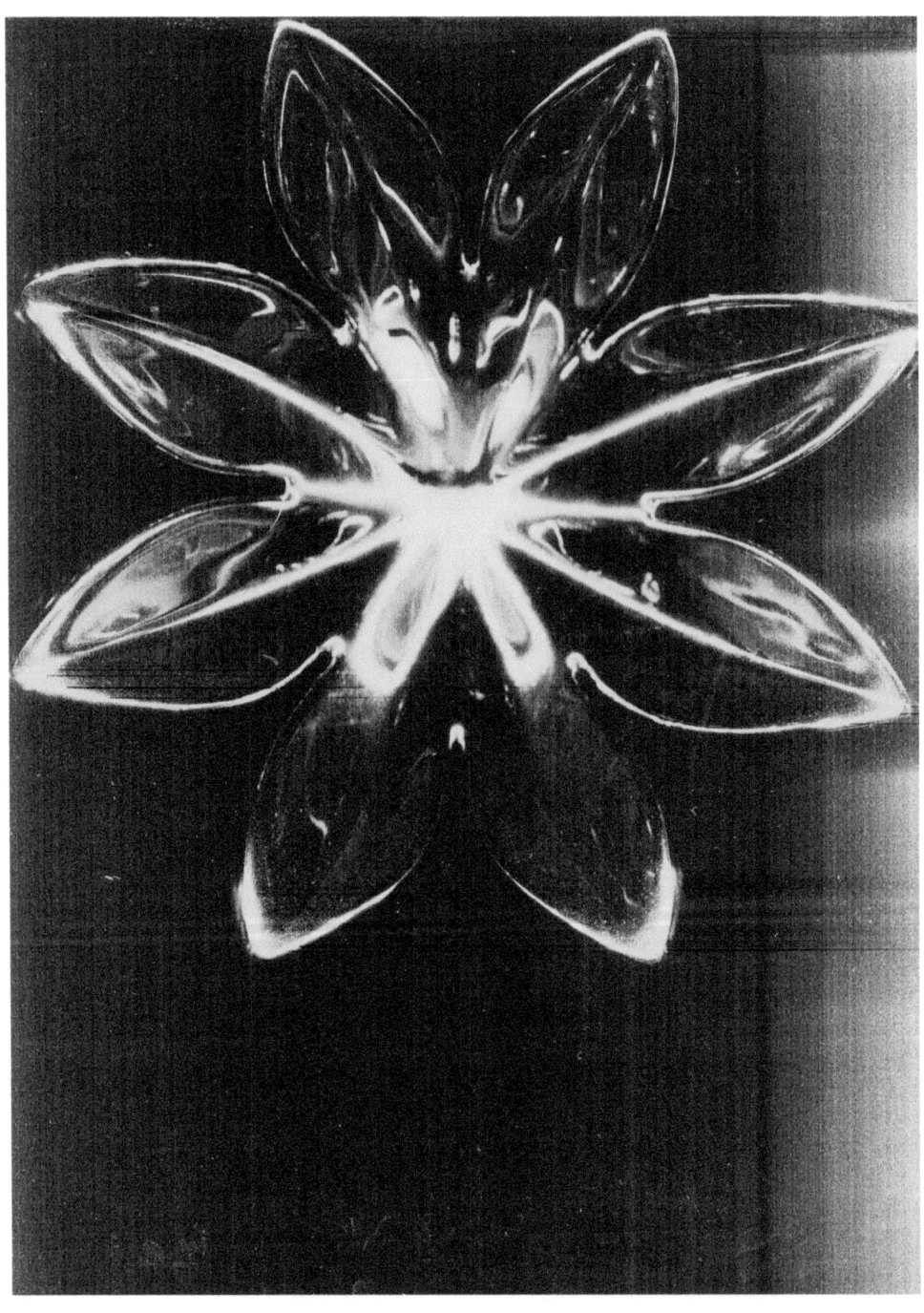

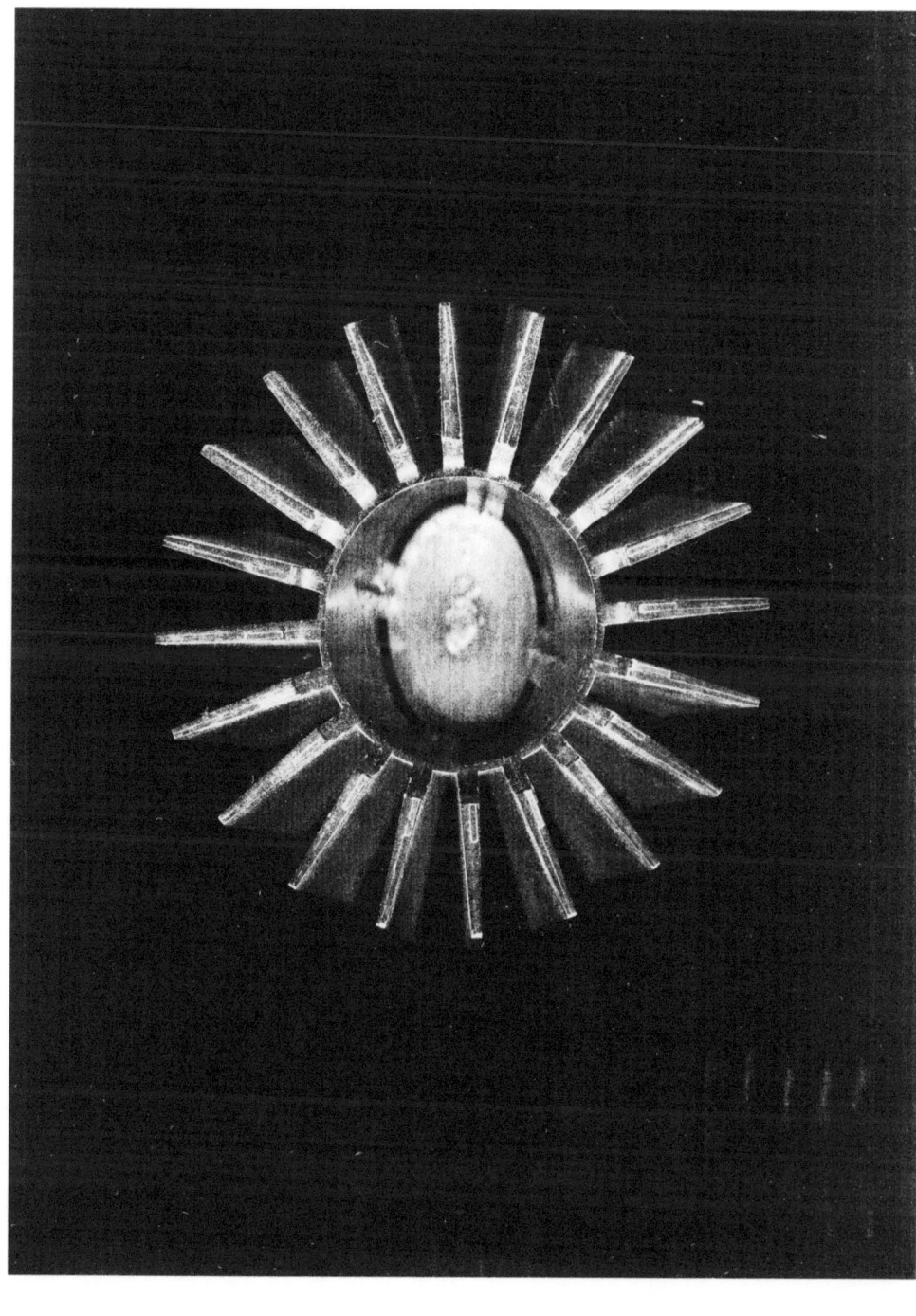

WE ARE ALL TIED TO OUR MEMORIES